W9-BSO-378

AN ATLAS OF
LATIN AMERICAN AFFAIRS

Other titles in the Praeger series
of world-affairs atlases

AN ATLAS OF WORLD AFFAIRS
  by Andrew Boyd

AN ATLAS OF AFRICAN AFFAIRS
  by Andrew Boyd and Patrick van Rensburg

AN ATLAS OF MIDDLE EASTERN AFFAIRS
  by Robert C. Kingsbury and Norman J. G. Pounds

AN ATLAS OF EUROPEAN AFFAIRS
  by Robert C. Kingsbury and Norman J. G. Pounds

AN ATLAS OF SOVIET AFFAIRS
  by Robert C. Kingsbury and Robert N. Taaffe

AN ATLAS OF
LATIN AMERICAN AFFAIRS

text by Ronald M. Schneider
maps by Robert C. Kingsbury

FREDERICK A. PRAEGER, *Publishers*
New York • Washington

BOOKS THAT MATTER

Published in the United States of America in 1965
by Frederick A. Praeger, Inc., Publishers
111 Fourth Avenue, New York, N.Y. 10003

Third printing, 1966

© 1965 by Frederick A. Praeger, Inc.

Library of Congress Catalog Card Number: Map 65-5

Maps 28, 44, and 51 incorporate information found
in Preston James, *Latin America* (3d ed.; New York:
The Odyssey Press). The authors gratefully acknowl-
edge the publisher's permission to use this material.

Printed in the United States of America

Contents

912.3
Sc359a

Foreword

Latin America is a large and diverse area whose importance has only recently been recognized in the United States as well as in Europe. Outsiders, who tend to impute to the region a uniformity which in reality does not exist, frequently judge Latin America as a whole on the basis of imperfect knowledge concerning one of its components. The Latin American countries have followed various paths toward modern nationhood, and the differences between nations are increasing rather than decreasing. In most important respects, "Latin American" is an artificial designation which is used by foreigners and which the area's inhabitants are either unaware of or seriously challenge. "Does Latin America exist?" is a question with which the intellectuals of these twenty-odd nations continue to wrestle. Meanwhile, their inhabitants are increasingly proud of their national identity and demand recognition as Brazilians, Mexicans, Argentines, Cubans, or Chileans. Resentment at being lumped together as "Latins" is far more intense than it was a generation ago. But, at the same time, there is a growing consciousness of common problems and the need for cooperation among countries by the better-informed and more active elements. Moreover, their world view is broadening to include the other developing nations in Africa, the Middle East, and Asia.

This atlas is intended as an aid to understanding this complex region, particularly the problem of its unity and diversity. Within the strict space limitations, historical, political, social, and economic information has been incorporated in the proportion the author considered best suited to this end. Both text and maps have been designed to lay a good foundation rather than to present an overwhelming mass of facts. Salient features have been emphasized, statistics rounded, and generalizations made wherever justified. The facts and figures come from a wide variety of sources, but the author takes full responsibility for their use and interpretation. Countries have been accorded space roughly in proportion to their populations, with the exceptions of the smaller islands of the Caribbean, which have been given more than population would merit, and Brazil, which has not been granted the third of the volume called for by its multiplying millions.

R. M. S.

New York
June, 1965

AN ATLAS OF
LATIN AMERICAN AFFAIRS

LATIN AMERICA AS A REGION

1. Geographical Factors

Latin America embraces the South American continent and that part of North America lying below the United States. The latter area is conventionally divided into Mexico, Central America, and the Caribbean. As indicated by the frequent use of the phrase "the twenty Latin American countries," there is no general agreement upon the inclusion in the region of those Caribbean islands often referred to as the West Indies, which historically have been European dependencies. Since several of these have recently become independent and are seeking admission to regional organizations, the problem of delimitation of the area is becoming increasingly complex and is no longer purely academic. The logic of economic and political developments, as well as geography, justifies the broader definition of the Latin American region used in this volume.

The land area of Latin America exceeds 7.9 million square miles, equal to that of Europe and the United States combined; South America alone accounts for 6.8 million square miles. Stretching 7,000 miles from north to south, or roughly the distance from London to Capetown, South America lies largely to the east of the United States; Lima and Santiago on the Pacific coast lie almost due south of Washington, D.C. At its easternmost point, it is within 1,600 nautical miles of Africa, and much of Latin America is as close or closer to Western Europe than it is to the United States—for example, Rio de Janeiro is closer to Lisbon than to New York. Most of the region lies within the tropics. Only Uruguay is located wholly within the temperate zone; Argentina, Chile, Mexico, and Paraguay also extend into it. Yet because of the high altitude of much of the area, relatively few Latin Americans live in tropical climes. In the highlands, above 5,000 feet, temperatures generally average below 65° F. Quito, situated almost on the equator, but at an altitude of over 9,000 feet, is uncomfortably cool, with an average temperature of 55° during the warmest month.

Geographically, Latin America is an exceedingly diverse area. One-fourth is mountainous, and an equal area is covered by tropical rain forests; another 10 per cent is desert or semi-arid. Less than 40 per cent is attractive to human habitation. In spite of the existence of four of the world's major river systems—the Amazon, La Plata, Orinoco, and Magdalena—the topography of South America is generally a barrier to transportation and commerce within countries, as well as between neighboring states. Indeed, despite their extensive land boundaries,

Areas over 5,000 feet above sea level shown are in solid black

most of the countries essentially face away from each other. Only in a few cases do national borders pass through heavily settled or even significantly developed areas.

2. Political Divisions

Of the twenty-two independent nations of Latin America, twenty are republics belonging to the Organization of American States and two are members of the British Commonwealth. In addition, the Caribbean subregion includes a variety of political entities enjoying differing degrees of independence as Departments of France, self-governing states under the Netherlands Crown, commonwealths associated with the United States, or dependent territories (see Map 24). These countries range from veritable subcontinents to small specks of coral, from emerging world powers to pale shadows of nationhood. Some have been independent for over 150 years, while others are still seeking to establish their sovereignty. Size and population are not necessarily correlated.

	Population (1965 est.)	Area in square miles	Persons per square mile
Latin America	243,725,000	7,924,497	31
Argentina	22,250,000	1,072,748	21
Bahamas	135,000	4,400	31
Barbados	280,000	166	1,686
Bolivia	4,285,000	424,163	10
Brazil	82,125,000	3,287,204	25
British Guiana	660,000	83,000	8
British Honduras	110,000	8,866	12
Chile	8,460,000	286,397	30
Colombia	17,020,000	439,813	39
Costa Rica	1,425,000	19,575	74
Cuba	7,455,000	44,218	169
Dominican Republic	3,575,000	18,816	190
Ecuador	5,200,000	104,506	50
El Salvador	2,850,000	8,164	348
French Guiana	35,000	35,135	1
Guadeloupe and Martinique	615,000	1,112	553
Guatemala	4,420,000	42,042	105
Haiti	4,610,000	10,714	430
Honduras	2,135,000	43,277	49
Jamaica	1,725,000	4,411	392
Leeward Islands	165,000	356	464
Mexico	40,650,000	760,375	54
Netherlands Antilles	230,000	341	620
Nicaragua	1,655,000	57,143	29
Panama	1,200,000	28,753	42
Paraguay	1,995,000	157,047	13
Peru	11,625,000	496,223	23
Puerto Rico	2,525,000	3,438	736
Surinam	375,000	55,144	7
Trinidad and Tobago	975,000	1,980	492

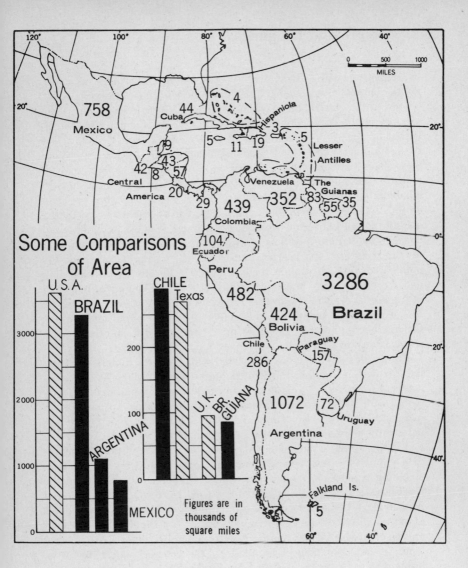

Some Comparisons of Area

Figures are in thousands of square miles

	Population (1965 est.)	Area in square miles	Persons per square mile
Uruguay	2,650,000	72,172	37
Venezuela	8,650,000	352,143	25
Virgin Islands	35,000	133	263
Windward Islands	400,000	825	485

5

3. People and Languages

In comparison with Africa, Asia, or even Europe, there is a very substantial linquistic homogeneity in Latin America. In eighteen countries, Spanish is the official language, and in most of these it is spoken by the majority of the population. Indian dialects are in common use only in Paraguay, the Andean highlands of Bolivia, Peru, and Ecuador, and the mountainous regions of Guatemala and southern Mexico. It is in these areas that the great majority of Latin America's more than 20 million unassimilated Indians live. Primitive Indians are almost the sole inhabitants of the vast four-country Amazon Basin (*compare the map on the opposite page with maps 5 and 60*). Portuguese is spoken by the one-third of all Latin Americans living in Brazil. English is widely used in the West Indies, as well as in British Guiana, but the dialect spoken by the working class in Jamaica is all but incomprehensible to the uninitiated. English also has some currency in Puerto Rico. In Surinam and the Netherlands Antilles, Dutch is the official language, but English is also spoken in the towns. French is the language taught in the schools of Haiti, as well as in Martinique, Guadeloupe, and French Guiana, but the tongue spoken in the city streets and countryside is a patois known as Creole.

Ethnic diversity is closely correlated with linguistic differences. Unlike the early settlers in the United States, relatively few of the colonizers of Latin America brought their families with them. Instead, they mated with Indian women. Hence the basic racial stock in most of the mainland countries is mestizo, or "mixed." European blood predominates only in such countries as Argentina, Uruguay, and Costa Rica, and in the southern part of Brazil, where there were no permanent Indian populations and where there was heavy European immigration, including women and children, during the nineteenth century. In the Caribbean and along the northern coast of Brazil, the heavy influx of African slaves led to a largely Negro population. Here the descendants of mixed alliances are called mulattoes, or, in the English-speaking areas, coloureds. Asiatics, mostly from India and Indonesia, are a major factor in the populations of Trinidad and the Guianas, where they were brought to work the plantations after the abolition of slavery. Japanese have recently become a significant element in parts of Brazil and coastal Peru.

The largest "white" component of the Latin American population today is not made up of descendants of the original colonizers, but instead dates from the heavy stream of European migration that began after independence had been won and lasted until the 1930's. Spain,

6

A. *Official languages:* 1—Spanish; 2—Portuguese; 3—English; 4—French; 5—Dutch

B. *Area where Indian languages are common*

Italy, Portugal, Germany, and Poland furnished the bulk of these immigrants; almost all settled below the Tropic of Capricorn.

7

4. Economic Development

Economically speaking, Latin America can best be described as a developing region. Its per capita annual income, roughly $325, is about one-ninth that enjoyed by the United States and only one-third the West European average. However, it compares quite favorably with the Middle East and is several times higher than the figures for Africa or Asia. Per capita income varies greatly within the region; there is a ten-to-one ratio between the extremes. In terms of growth rates, the regional economy showed an average annual gain of 4.7 per cent during the decade of the 1950's, but this progress was again very uneven from one country to another. Among the major countries, Venezuela, Brazil, and Mexico were growing at well over 6 per cent annually, while the economies of Chile, Peru, and Argentina were expanding at only a fraction of that speed. Since 1960, Brazil, however, has slowed down markedly, while Peru has gained momentum. In the countries with high rates of population increase, much of the yearly economic expansion is offset by the larger number of mouths to be fed (see Map 60).

But per capita income levels and annual growth rates are only crude indicators of standards of living within the various Latin American countries. In some, a small elite receives an exceedingly high proportion of the national income, while in others a relatively balanced occupational structure, taxation, and social-welfare programs have led to a more even distribution of wealth. Almost without exception, however, rural levels of living—in health, education, housing, and nutrition—are far below those of the urban areas, including slums. Nearly half the total population of Latin America still live at the subsistence level and are on the margin of national social, economic, and political life.

In general, the larger and more populous countries of Latin America have begun to pull away from the lesser states in terms of economic development. This is particularly evident in the industrial realm. Brazil, despite its large rural population and a relatively late start in industrializing, has become the leading manufacturing country of Latin America. Mexico, which has paid greater attention to its rural areas and to social justice, has shown perhaps the most sustained and balanced economic development of any Latin American country. Argentina, which was first to establish the basis for economic "take-off," but has tended to stagnate in recent years, still supports one of the region's highest living standards and one in which most of the population participates. Venezuela has made very substantial strides during the past seven years in spreading the benefits of its high oil revenues more widely. Chile and, to a lesser extent, Colombia are also above the region's average in eco-

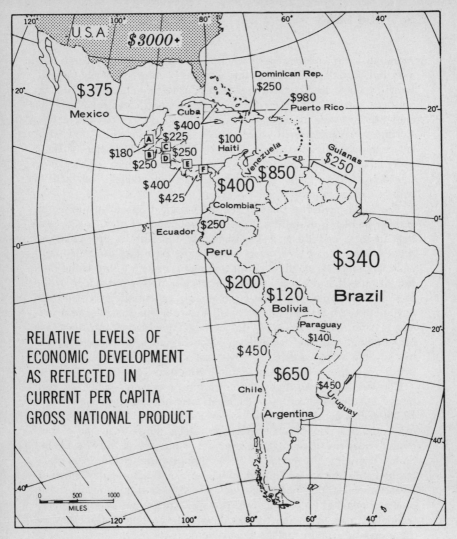

Central American Countries: A—Guatemala; B—El Salvador; C—Honduras; D—Nicaragua; E—Costa Rica; F—Panama

nomic terms, as is Cuba, despite an absolute as well as relative decline since the Castro regime took over. Peru is the only major Latin American country which has lagged behind in economic development; it is also the only one of these eight with a large Indian population which has not been integrated into the money economy.

9

5. The Land

Although Latin America has nearly 8 million square miles of land, only a relatively small proportion of this area has been productively utilized. Large expanses are too dry, rugged, cold, or infertile for agriculture. In northern Mexico, along the coasts of Peru and northern Chile, throughout most of western and southern Argentina, and in part of the Brazilian Northeast, only scattered oases can be successfully cultivated without expensive irrigation works. Indeed, the major proportion of Latin America's increased agricultural production during recent years can be traced to Mexican gains resulting from massive national investment in widespread irrigation projects.

The Andes comprise some of the most rugged terrain in the world, and the highlands of eastern Brazil, the mountains of Mexico and Central America, and the volcanic islands of the Antilles are almost as rugged. Products of these areas which must be transported to distant markets must have high value for volume in order to absorb the high freight rates that result from the construction and maintenance of the few roads and railroads. Other large areas of potentially good land still have not been put to productive use because of the difficulty of access and expense of settlement. With increased population pressures (*see Map 60*) and improved technology, however, much of the area labeled too infertile or too isolated on the accompanying map will be incorporated into the economic life of South America.

Contrary to popular myth, little of Latin America is too hot for habitation and development. Indeed, even near the equator, land above 12,000 feet is generally too cold for normal farming. Throughout tropical Latin America, temperatures are rarely higher than those commonly encountered during the summer in broad areas of the United States. Humidity, the monotony of continuous warm weather, and easily leached soils are instead the drawbacks to agricultural development. As recent experience in mineral-rich areas such as the Maracaibo Basin of Venezuela and the Brazilian territory of Amapá has shown, modern technology can overcome the handicaps of the humid tropics when the economic promise justifies the expense.

So far, Latin American development has been concentrated in relatively small islands of productivity separated by seas of scrub brush and grassland, dense tropical forests, and mountain barriers. Moreover, ownership of much of the best land—even in heavily populated areas near the urban markets—is in the hands of a small but politically powerful class, while the majority of those who work the land do not receive an income sufficient to give them significant purchasing power. On

1—high mountains; *2*—sparsely populated (fewer than 2–3 persons per square mile)

grounds of both social justice and economic desirability, Mexico, Bolivia, Venezuela, and Cuba introduced basic reforms in their land-tenure patterns prior to 1960, and after the launching of the Alliance for Progress in 1961 most of the rest began to follow suit.

6.   Foreign Investment

Foreign capital has played a major part in the development of Latin America, but its future role is now a major political issue in many countries. Prior to 1929, there was a heavy flow of foreign private investment into Latin America. A situation developed in which the United States was not only the principal purchaser of the region's mineral exports, but was also deeply involved financially in their exploitation. Similarly, British capital was heavily invested in the Argentine livestock industry. During the world depression of the 1930's, there was a net outflow of foreign capital (repatriated profits, etc., exceeded new investment). In the years after World War II, the renewed stream of capital to the area exceeded $750 million a year, and by 1959 direct foreign investment totaled almost $14 billion, three-fifths from the United States. Private foreign investment has fallen off as a result of the Castro regime's wholesale expropriation of foreign capital and political instability accompanied by threats of expropriation elsewhere. Indeed, repatriated earnings exceed the flow of new U.S. capital to the area in 1962. Since then, public funds and loans from international agencies have at least partially filled the gap.

Most of U.S. private investment in Latin America is in the extractive and public-utility fields: 37 per cent in petroleum, 13 per cent in mining, and 8.5 per cent in transportation, communications, and power. (The last area is down sharply as a result of Cuban expropriations and Mexican and Brazilian government purchases of power companies.) Only 22 per cent is in manufacturing, the field which Latin Americans associate most directly with economic development. Geographical concentration is also great, with 33 per cent of U.S. Latin American investment in Venezuela, 13 per cent in Brazil, 10 per cent in Mexico, and 9 per cent each in Argentina and Chile.

Widespread Latin American reservations about the value of private foreign investment rest upon the belief that exploitation of nonrenewable resources should be in national hands; that excessive profits are being remitted by foreign firms; that foreign capital perpetuates "colonial" economic relationships and discourages development and diversification; and that foreign companies meddle in domestic politics and then seek the protection of their home government when their interests clash with those of the host country. Relatively few working-class Latin Americans are convinced that they should pay substantially for the technical know-how of foreign firms, that profits should be high because of the risks involved, and that foreign investment creates new jobs and opportunities for advancement. Many Latin Americans do realize that the region lacks the capital to develop its own resources,

1 areas where many large estates have been subdivided; 2—areas where widespread government expropriations of property have occurred

but they greatly prefer government-to-government loans. For this reason, they find the Alliance for Progress more satisfactory than previous U.S. policy. To be welcome, foreign investment must increasingly conform to the developmental aspirations of the Latin Americans.

7. Mineral Wealth

The quest for gold and silver provided much of the impetus for the exploitation and settlement of Latin America, and during the colonial epoch the region—particularly Mexico, Peru, and Brazil—provided most of the world's supply of precious metals and gems. Although the emphasis has shifted to industrial metals and petroleum, minerals still play an important role in the region's economic life and foreign trade. Oil alone accounts for about 25 per cent of Latin American exports, but almost all of this comes from one country, Venezuela. Metallic ores and other minerals, such as nitrate and sulfur, account for an additional 10 per cent.

Mineral deposits are distributed quite widely throughout the region; only Uruguay, Paraguay, and Central America appear short-changed. Mining is relatively most important in the Andean countries: copper, iron, and nitrates in Chile; tin in Bolivia; lead, copper, silver, zinc, and iron in Peru; and iron ore on the largest scale of all in Venezuela, where the deposits are part of the Guiana highlands. Mexico's mountains also yield lead, silver, copper, and iron in major quantities. Oil basins are found adjacent to these mountain areas in Venezuela, Mexico, Colombia, Argentina, and Peru. The last four countries, together with Brazil, have additional fuel resources in the form of coal, also essential for their growing steel industries. Brazil's mineral wealth is largely in iron and manganese. With a limited supply of petroleum for an industrializing nation, Brazil has instead utilized its almost limitless hydroelectric potential. It has also explored the possibilities for commercial exploitation of its extensive deposits of oil-bearing shale and continues to investigate the peaceful uses of atomic energy, particularly in the generation of electric power. The Guianas and Jamaica contain valuable deposits of bauxite (aluminum ore), and recent reports indicate that Costa Rica may also become a commercial producer of this increasingly utilized mineral.

Although Latin America's mineral resources are substantial, they probably do not exceed those of other comparable areas. In many cases, large mineral exports are linked with low internal demand. As the region's economic development continues, these minerals will be consumed on a much larger scale. Brazil and Argentina may provide a growing market for Venezuela's oil, but the latter will long continue as a major world supplier. It is also evident that Venezuela and Brazil have enough iron to increase exports sharply as North American and European resources are depleted. Moreover, there are vast areas of the South American interior which have not yet been prospected and which may contain additional mineral riches. In some Latin American

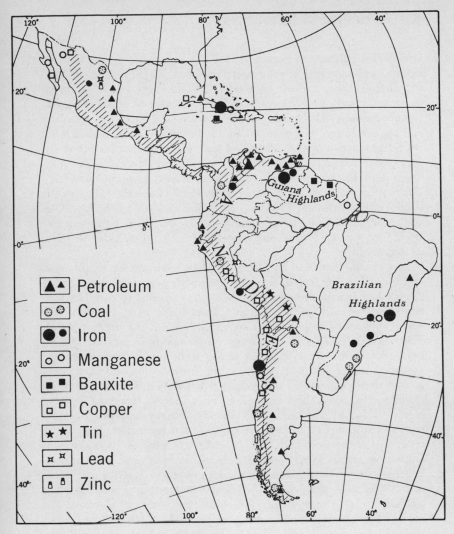

▲▲	Petroleum
⊙⊛	Coal
●●	Iron
○○	Manganese
■■	Bauxite
□□	Copper
★★	Tin
⋈⋈	Lead
▯▯	Zinc

Main mountain areas are shaded

countries, national restrictions on foreign exploitation of mineral reserves have delayed, temporarily at least, the development of these resources.

15

8. Agricultural Resources

Over half the Latin American labor force is engaged in agriculture and livestock raising, yet this sector contributes only 20 per cent of the total economic product. Agricultural productivity has lagged badly in recent years, and a large proportion of rural dwellers are still engaged in subsistence farming. The great part of agricultural production goes into feeding the burgeoning populations of the cities. Thus, with a total annual production of over 25 million tons, corn does not feature in export trade. Wheat is sold to Europe, but not because the region produces more than it consumes. Brazil must import huge amounts from U.S. surplus stocks made available under Public Law 480. The same is largely true of livestock. Brazil has 80 million head of cattle, 50 million hogs, and 20 million sheep, among the highest such figures in the world, but it is not a significant exporter of meat, wool, hides, or other related products.

Most Latin American countries produce cash export crops upon which they depend heavily for badly needed foreign exchange. During the colonial period, the region specialized in tropical foodstuffs which could not be cultivated in Europe. Thus sugar, cocoa, cotton, and spices were raised on plantations in northern Brazil and the Caribbean. Elsewhere, livestock was introduced on the natural pastures. The labor needs of the plantations led to the institution of Negro slavery; ranching needed few workers. With the urbanization and population growth that accompanied the Industrial Revolution, the European demand for imported meat and grain rose sharply. Ranching became highly profitable, and the rich grasslands of Argentina and Uruguay were put to the plow to raise wheat and corn for export. During the latter part of the nineteenth century, coffee emerged as the major agricultural export of many Latin American countries, and subsequently bananas came to be of prime importance in Central America and Ecuador. At the same time, the United States emerged as a major trading partner. Today, coffee, sugar, and cotton trail only petroleum as the region's leading exports (accounting, respectively, for 20, 10, and 4 per cent of sales abroad), with meat, hides, cocoa, wheat, wool, tobacco, and corn making up an additional 10 per cent.

Paradoxically, many countries of Latin America must import foodstuffs or experience acute shortages. Most of the densely populated West Indian islands devote nearly all their tillable land to export crops, which in good years can pay for food imports in excess of their own productive capacity. But loss of markets to new African competition or a drop in commodity prices can completely disrupt this type of economy. Price fluctuations pose a severe problem even to the more devel-

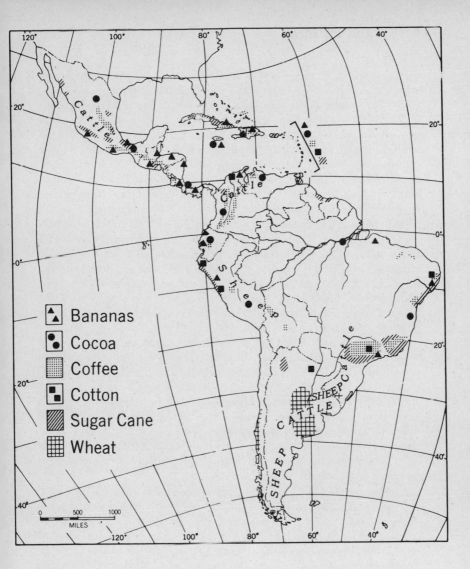

oped and diversified economies of South America. For example, in
1958 sugar and wool prices both fell more than 25 per cent. Coffee
overproduction has become a chronic problem, although in recent years
some progress has been made in commodity price stabilization through
such measures as the International Coffee Agreement of 1962, in which
both producing and consuming nations participate.

9. Trade Patterns

The pattern of Latin America's international commerce, although slowly changing, still reflects the area's traditional position as a supplier of foodstuffs and raw materials to the more industrialized nations of the Western world. Thus the United States purchases about one-half of all Latin American exports, paying over $4 billion each year for petroleum, coffee, copper, lead, sugar, cacao, tin, and a variety of other commodities. Slightly over 30 per cent of Latin America's export trade is with Western Europe, particularly Great Britain. The British have long provided a market for Argentine and Uruguayan meat, hides, wool, and wheat, and are committed to taking the major portion of the exports of their Commonwealth cousins in Jamaica, Trinidad, and British Guiana. Nearly 15 per cent of the region's foreign commerce is with Japan and the Communist countries. Japan makes substantial purchases of cotton, wool, and sugar; the limited trade of most countries with the Soviet bloc is relatively diversified including some coffee, wool, wheat, and minerals. Since 1959, Cuba has come to trade largely with the Soviet Union, Communist China, and Eastern Europe, but this is for political rather than economic reasons.

There is relatively little trade among Latin American countries, since most are food and raw-material exporters with basically competitive economies. Only four countries have regularly carried on more than 10 per cent of their trade with their neighbors. Paraguay is in many respects an economic satellite of Argentina, while British Guiana supplies rice to the sugar-producing islands of the West Indies. Venezuela ships much of its petroleum to the refineries of Curaçao, Aruba, and Trinidad, and some to oil-hungry Brazil. Over one-half of intraregional trade is in foodstuffs and one-fourth in fuels. Exchange of manufactured goods on an important scale is only beginning.

During the past five years, the countries of Latin America have paid increasing attention to the possibilities of greater regional trade and economic integration. In 1961, the Latin American Free Trade Association (LAFTA) came into being. Numbering among its members all the South American countries except Bolivia and Venezuela (although the latter is expected to join eventually), plus Mexico, LAFTA has worked toward the progressive lowering of tariff walls. Yet, under present plans, at least another decade will be needed before essentially free trade is achieved. A Central American Common Market has also been evolving in a relatively satisfactory manner; since its formation in 1960, intraregional commerce has risen from 3 to almost 15 per cent of the total international trade of these countries. For the LAFTA coun-

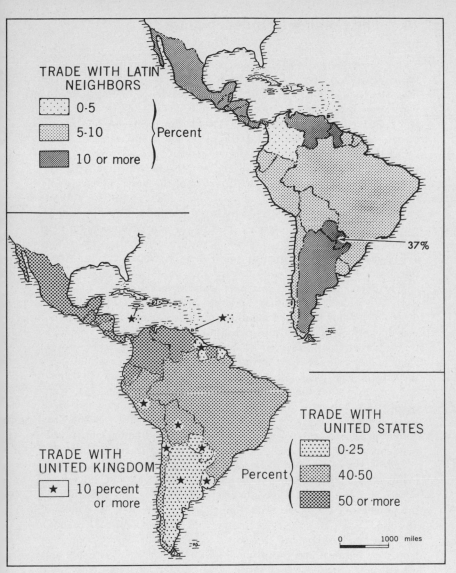

TRADE WITH LATIN
NEIGHBORS
- 0-5
- 5-10 } Percent
- 10 or more }

37%

TRADE WITH
UNITED STATES
- 0-25
- 40-50 } Percent
- 50 or more

TRADE WITH
UNITED KINGDOM
- ★ 10 percent
  or more

0   1000 miles

Upper map shows percentage of total foreign trade of each Latin American country that is carried on with other Latin American countries; lower map shows percentage carried on with the United States and the United Kingdom

tries the comparable figures are 6.8 per cent in 1960 and 10 per cent in 1964, or from $715 million to $1.1 billion in four years.

10. The Coming of Independence

Young in comparison with the countries of Europe, but old in relation to those of Africa or Asia, most of the Latin American nations have been in existence for about 150 years. The independence of Latin America was closely bound up with the Napoleonic Wars. The first wave of revolt coincided with the placing of Joseph Bonaparte on the Spanish throne, and only gradually did complete independence from Spain, rather than restoration of the legitimate monarch, come to be the dominant objective. The wars that took place in the decade after 1810 were as much civil wars as revolutions. Leaders of the independence movements came largely from the elite of those born in the New World (*criollos*), a group long frustrated by its lack of influence in the administration of the colonies. Armies, both royal and revolutionary, were quite small, and no battle involved more than a few thousand troops.

The main struggle in Spanish South America was led by the Argentine José de San Martín, who crossed the Andes and liberated Chile, and by Simón Bolívar, whose armies won the independence of what is today Venezuela, Colombia, Ecuador, Peru, and Bolivia. Bolívar's dream of holding this area together in one great nation or federation was doomed by distance, regionalism, and political rivalries. A similar fragmentation took place in Central America, where independence came almost without effort in the wake of Mexico's successful declaration. In the Caribbean, Haiti broke away from France in 1804, but it was not until 1898 that Cuba threw off the Spanish yoke; the British colonies are only now becoming independent. Brazil, elevated to co-equal status with Portugal after the imperial court sought asylum from Napoleon, was able to sever its ties peacefully and embark upon independence under a monarchy, a system it did not abandon until 1889.

Independence had little effect on the lives of the great mass of the population. The economic and social order was largely unchanged, and politics in the decades following independence was almost exclusively the province of the upper-class elites. Large landowners, the military, and the Church quickly consolidated their control, although in some of the economically more developed countries they were soon challenged by business and professional groups which were generally anticlerical and opposed to militarism. The former led the Conservative parties; the latter founded Liberal parties. In some countries, the question of how the country would be organized—federalism versus centralism—was the central political issue and one that was often settled by force of arms. Indeed, the Liberals were compelled to fight their way to power more frequently than not and were at times ousted by armed revolt. In very few countries was the ballot box accepted as the final

Approximate dates of independence or freedom from European colonial domination are shown; heavy line indicates the routes of the military campaigns of Bolívar

political arbiter before the end of the first century of independence. During this period, dictatorships alternated with periods of instability, and the frequent revolutions were almost devoid of social content.

11. Twentieth-Century Politics

The twenty-odd independent Latin American countries have each adopted republican forms of government and constitutions generally modeled after that of the United States; few, however, have gone very far toward becoming stable, mature, representative democracies. All are on the way to becoming modern nation-states and are undergoing substantial political change, reflecting in part the economic development and social upheaval which have characterized the area in recent decades. The pace and extent of this political change vary greatly from country to country: some nations have experienced revolutions which have toppled the old elites and elevated new groups to dominant positions; others are still characterized by semifeudal power configurations and social orders. Generalizations are therefore hazardous, unless so carefully qualified as to have little meaning. Certainly political life in much of the area is still highly personalistic, but in a number of the larger and more advanced nations there has been a significant development of broadly based and relatively impersonal political institutions. The need to curb the most divisive effects of unrestrained competition until a sufficient political consensus may develop has led several countries to impose some form of institutional restraint, yet these same nations may have the broadest effective political participation. Except in rare cases, black and white categories, such as "democracy" or "dictatorship," are of little value. Thus the accompanying map can give only a crude indication of the political situation in the several republics. Moreover, the political development of these countries rarely moves in a straight line, and temporary setbacks occur frequently along the road to viable representative systems.

While the traditional Conservative and Liberal parties still exist in many Latin American republics, in only a few, most notably Colombia, are they the major contenders for political power. Even before World War I, Radical and Socialist parties emerged to enrich political life in those countries with the most extensive industrialization, urbanization, and immigration. In Argentina and Chile, the Radicals soon came to share control of at least the national government. The interwar period saw the beginnings of a variety of Social Democratic parties, with the American Popular Revolutionary Alliance (APRA) in Peru as a prototype. This period also saw the establishment of a broad-based official party in Mexico—a major step in institutionalizing the national revolution which in overthrowing the old order in 1910 had inaugurated two decades of civil strife.

In the postwar period, there have been several swings of the political pendulum. The Great Depression tended to breed dictatorships, but in

May 1965

HAITI
DOMINICAN REP.

GUATEMALA
EL SALVADOR
PANAMA

Number of successful coups or revolutions since 1950

BOLIVIA

CHILE

PARAGUAY

URUGUAY

CUBA

HONDURAS
NICARAGUA

MEXICO

VENEZUELA

COSTA RICA
COLOMBIA

ECUADOR

BRAZIL

PERU

May 1955

ARGENTINA

1
2
3
4

0   1000   2000 miles

1—elected constitutional regime; 2—provisional government resulting from a coup, revolution, or assassination; 3—dictatorship; 4—colonial possessions and nonindependent states

the immediate postwar years civilian reform governments replaced a number of traditional authoritarian regimes. Disillusionment with attempts at quick and at times radical solutions to basic socio-economic problems spurred the way for a series of more conservative administrations, often run by the military. Beginning with the fall of Argentine dictator Juan Perón in 1955, these strongmen were toppled and succeeded by representative civilian governments. The 1962–64 period witnessed a new wave of military coups, which came to embrace eight countries in two years.

Once again Argentina was the bellwether as the government of President Arturo Frondizi transgressed the boundaries laid down by the armed forces in its effort to reincorporate the Peronist masses. In mid-1962, the Peruvian military seized power when electoral results seemed to be favoring the APRA presidential candidate. In a seven-month period in 1963, Miguel Ydígoras in Guatemala, Carlos Arosemena in Ecuador, Ramón Villeda Morales in Honduras, and Juan Bosch in the Dominican Republic were ousted by military coups. In April, 1964, the erratically leftist regime of João Goulart in Brazil was swept from power by the armed forces, supported by a majority of state governors. Bolivia's floundering national revolution, headed by Victor Paz Estenssoro, was toppled in November after more than twelve years in power. While in Argentina and Peru democratically elected regimes took office within little more than a year, in the other six countries very limited progress has been made toward a return to constitutionality.

Political life in most of the American republics has been enriched in recent decades by the emergence of new political forces stemming from urbanization and industrialization. In many countries—including the largest and the most important—a sizable middle class and an urban proletariat have evolved and given rise to new political movements to challenge the entrenched elites. In several countries, political leadership has passed into their hands, and parties long identified with propertied groups have been forced to tailor their appeals to the aspirations of the white-collar employees and to promise greater social-welfare benefits to organized labor. And as the social composition of the officer corps has broadened, the military is no longer the handmaiden of the oligarchs. The Church, too, has increasingly sought to end its identification with the established order. Generals and bishops are now found on the side of change and reform as frequently as they are aligned in support of the *status quo*.

Although the groups working for representative democracy are stronger than ever before, the struggle for freedom and justice is far from won. Several traditional dictators still remain in power (although only in relatively small nations), and in Cuba a traditional authoritarian regime has been followed by a totalitarian revolution, a mass-based

24

dictatorship allied with the Soviet Union. In many countries, too, sizable segments of the population are becoming alienated from the established political systems as their demands for a voice in national decision-making are not heeded. Pressures for sweeping change appear to be irresistible in the long run, and the political institutions of some countries may lack the strength and flexibility to accommodate this change.

Violence is still a significant factor of political life in much of the region. In fourteen countries, governments have been overthrown by force since 1950, and in most cases such unscheduled presidential changes have taken place two or three times in the past fifteen years. In two other republics, Nicaragua and Paraguay, entrenched dictatorial regimes have withstood repeated uprisings during this period. Moreover, in the course of the last decade four Latin American political strongmen have been assassinated: José Remón in Panama (1955), Anastasio Somoza in Nicaragua (1956), Carlos Castillo Armas in Guatemala (1957), and Rafael Trujillo in the Dominican Republic (1961). In recent years, leftist guerrilla bands and terrorist organizations have been a common feature of the political life in Venezuela, Guatemala, Nicaragua, Peru, Bolivia, Colombia, and Argentina, and sporadic activity has occurred elsewhere. Exile invasions have repeatedly taken place in Paraguay and Haiti, where terror is a mainstay of the durable dictators.

Political democratization and stability may well accompany continued economic development and social reform, but experience indicates that this will be far from automatic. The emerging masses must be convinced that their demands for a better life can and will be fulfilled through representative political processes. In such countries as Venezuela, Chile, and Mexico, they appear to have some faith in this possibility. In other parts of the region, the question remains very much in doubt. Aspirations continue to outrun achievement, and particularistic interests frequently prevail over national needs.

12.   Regions and the Revolution

With an area of over 760,000 square miles, Mexico is the world's ninth largest country. As New Spain, it was the administrative capital and economic center for a region stretching from Oregon to Panama and embracing the Caribbean and the Philippines. Within its present boundaries are found a number of distinctive regions, which only in recent years have been knit into an integrated nation. Geography has proven to be a barrier to this transformation; it required one of the most thorough and prolonged national revolutions of the twentieth century to turn Mexico into a modern nation.

Mexico's twenty-nine states, Federal District, and two territories fall naturally into four geo-economic divisions. The northern three-fifths of the country is essentially an arid region, much like western Texas, New Mexico, and Arizona. Ranching predominates on this 3,000–4,000 foot-high plateau, and on the slopes of the mountains bordering it on both sides. Irrigation projects make farming possible, and recent national administrations have invested considerable amounts in the construction of such works. Indeed, nearly three-fourths of the more than 7.5 million acres brought into production through irrigation has been done since 1947. Several multipurpose basin development commissions have contributed to the development of these oases. Urbanization and limited industrialization are changing the lives of many of the nearly one-fourth of the country's population who inhabit this region. This is particularly true of the northeastern corner and the Gulf coast oilfields.

Central Mexico, with about one-fifth of the nation's territory, is the heartland of the country. Here, in a series of high-altitude basins, live 60 per cent of the Mexican people. Its western portion is distinguished by a relative absence of the large estates and landless peasant masses which characterized much of rural Mexico. The humid and rugged South, lying close to the Pacific coast, contains much of Indian Mexico. Its agricultural and livestock production helps feed the central region, particularly the urban core in the Valley of Mexico. It also furnishes coffee and cocoa for export. The flat, forested, and rainy Yucatán peninsula is the least productive of Mexico's regions. Like the South, it contains roughly one-tenth of the country's area and population.

Equally as essential as these geographical factors to an appreciation of Mexico is an understanding of its revolution. Following independence from Spain, which was a profoundly conservative reaction in contrast to South America, Mexico experimented with a monarchy under a local creole before falling into a prolonged period of instability dur-

ing which war with the United States over Texas cost the country nearly half its territory. A liberal reform movement in the late 1850's was set back by French intervention and the establishment of a puppet Mexican Empire under Maximilian of Austria. In 1866, the French withdrew, and the Liberals, under Benito Juárez, regained power. After the death of the great Mexican patriot, the Presidency was occupied by Porfirio Díaz, who remained in power for more than three decades, beginning in 1876. Díaz betrayed the precepts of his mentor and established a highly centralized dictatorship which largely ignored the welfare of the great majority of the Mexican people. The economic development of the country was achieved through foreign investment, in partnership with a small Europeanized elite, and at an excessive price. Thus the stage was set for the revolution, which began in late 1910 and produced the governmental institutions in effect today (*see Map 17*).

13. The Northern Border

That part of Mexico bordering the United States bears more than a physical resemblance to the U.S. Southwest. Throughout the colonial period the areas were jointly administered, and U.S. incorporation of what was once half of Mexico's national territory took place only a little over a century ago. Indeed, territorial adjustments are still being made, as was the case of the Chamizal, a square mile of land lying between El Paso and Ciudad Juárez, settled by treaty in mid-1964. The cultural border between Mexico and the United States cannot be reduced to a line on a map, since from Texas to California the heritage of Mexican rule remains in place names, and persons of Mexican ancestry make up a significant proportion of the population. Such influences are reinforced by the annual influx of Mexican harvest workers (*braceros*) and illegal immigrants (wetbacks), as well as by the steady stream of U.S. tourists, numbering in the tens of thousands, to such border cities as Tijuana, Mexicali, Nogales, Nuevo Laredo, and Ciudad Juárez. The $800 million spent by these tourists amounts to about 40 per cent of Mexico's total foreign-exchange earnings. In the future, the two countries will probably influence each other over a much wider area, as vacationers from north of the Rio Grande penetrate to Mexico City, Acapulco, and Mérida, and Mexican farm laborers work their way a thousand miles into the United States. In addition, an increasing number of students choose to study in their neighboring country, and a growing number of North Americans are spending their retirement years in Mexico, where the favorable exchange rate (roughly, 12 pesos to the dollar) helps to stretch pension checks.

The United States and Mexico share many common problems. The way in which a U.S. city disposes of its sewage can be of major concern to its Mexican neighbors. Conversely, Tijuana's wide-open nightlife presents problems for California authorities. Many Mexican communities are dependent upon streams and rivers originating in the United States. In recent years, a number of major power and irrigation facilities have been constructed as joint efforts; for example, the Falcón Dam on the Rio Grande has turned the once almost desert area between Brownsville-Matamoros and El Paso–Ciudad Juárez into a highly productive agricultural region. While relations between the two countries generally have been good, and are improving as both national governments play a more constructive role, local friction over such matters as sin, salinity, and sewage will probably continue.

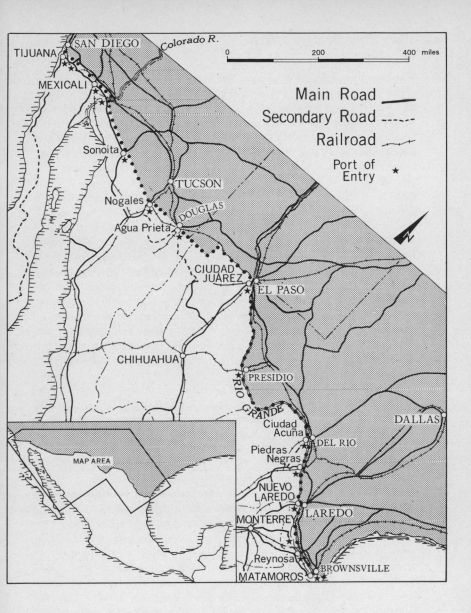

14. People and Cities

Mexico's population of 40 million, growing at the rate of over 1 million a year, is second only to that of Brazil in Latin America. Immigration has played a relatively small role, either during the late colonial period or after independence; rather, the people of Mexico are descended largely from the relatively advanced Indian civilizations predating the conquest. The last of these, the Aztecs, had extended their empire, ruled from what is now Mexico City, over much of the Mexican plateau. Thus the Spanish adventurers who arrived in 1519 found a situation much like the one their colleagues were to encounter in Peru a decade later (*see Map* 38). Hernán Cortés and his followers opened the way for colonization by a small number of Europeans, chiefly Spanish, who dominated a sizable Indian labor force engaged in mining and agriculture. Thus, while about 60 per cent of the modern Mexican people are mestizo, the European component of this mixture is relatively low. Less than 15 per cent of Mexico's population still live "Indian-style," and not all of these speak an Indian language. The "white" segment of the population, estimated at 15 per cent, is concentrated in the cities, where it is still the dominant element of the upper and professional classes. The position of the old rural upper class was largely destroyed by the revolution, but a majority of the remaining landowners are white.

Mexico is quite deeply split between the rural and village sector—responsible for the country's fairly high production of basic foodstuffs, such as corn, beans, and wheat, as well as some livestock production—and the rapidly growing urban sector. One-third of all Mexicans now live in towns and cities of more than 25,000, and the subregional centers, with populations ranging up to 100,000, are in many cases the country's fastest-growing communities. There are already about fifteen cities with between 100,000 and 200,000 inhabitants, in addition to the five larger urban centers and one major metropolitan area.

Mexico City, whose population has quadrupled since 1940, is one of the world's great metropolises. With more than 5 million inhabitants, it is the political, administrative, financial, commercial, industrial, and cultural capital of the country. Situated in a basin at an elevation of 7,500 feet, it is largely built upon land once covered by lakes; hence it is slowly settling. Its year-round favorable climate is suitable for sustained effort; the city is experiencing a construction boom, and modern supermarkets and department stores fill their shelves with locally produced articles which are quickly bought by the relatively affluent mass of consumers. Numerically, the burgeoning middle class and factory

30

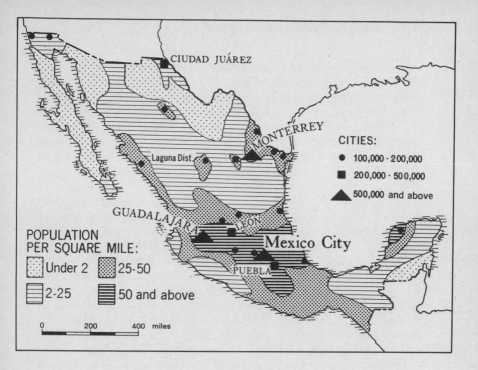

CIUDAD JUÁREZ

MONTERREY

CITIES:
- ● 100,000 - 200,000
- ■ 200,000 - 500,000
- ▲ 500,000 and above

Laguna Dist.

GUADALAJARA

LEÓN

Mexico City

PUEBLA

POPULATION PER SQUARE MILE:
- Under 2
- 2-25
- 25-50
- 50 and above

0   200   400   miles

workers make up as large a proportion of the population as in any Latin American city, including Buenos Aires and São Paulo, and their purchasing power is roughly equivalent.

Guadalajara, which boasts a population of nearly 700,000, has been Mexico's number-two urban center since colonial days. Monterrey, the country's third largest city, with about 600,000 inhabitants, is the hub of Mexico's steel industry and the major industrial complex outside the capital. Puebla, with nearly 300,000 inhabitants, is the heart of the country's textile industry; Ciudad Juárez, only slightly smaller, is the most important of the border cities. León has recently moved ahead as the largest of the several provincial centers near the Mexico City–Guadalajara axis. Veracruz and Tampico are the country's chief ports; Mazatlán, on the Pacific coast, plays a lesser role.

15. Agriculture and Mining

Agrarian reform has been a touchstone of the Mexican revolution. Under the Díaz regime, nearly all arable land was concentrated in the hands of a small number of landowners, whose sprawling haciendas often swallowed up land which had traditionally belonged to Indian communities. Most of the mestizo population had been reduced to virtual serfdom through a vicious system of debt peonage. In the years between the promulgation of the 1917 constitution, which established the legal basis for sweeping agrarian reforms, and 1934, nearly 20 million acres were expropriated and distributed, largely to indigenous communities in the form of *ejidos,* or communal holdings. President Lázaro Cárdenas (1934–40) accelerated the program, distributing 41 million acres. His three successors, increasingly concerned with industrialization and urban problems, in eighteen years issued titles to 38 million acres. Under Adolfo López Mateos (1958–64), the program was revitalized, and another 40 million acres were distributed. Thus, in less than fifty years one-third of the total area of the country has been taken from the old dominant class and reallocated to the rural masses—an impressive achievement. At the same time, production of most important foodstuffs has been increased, making the country largely self-sufficient in this field.

Mining, for many years the mainstay of the export economy, still makes an important contribution. Although silver production has decreased since independence, Mexico's widely scattered mines still account for about one-fourth of world production; gold is also produced in significant amounts. In the twentieth century, industrial metals have become increasingly important to Mexico, if not to the world market. Lead production accounts for nearly half the Latin American total and is valued at over $50 million annually, a figure which is matched by zinc production. Copper, manganese, sulfur, uranium and mercury are of somewhat less importance. Fortunately for an industrializing country, Mexico has both iron ore and coal in abundance—at least 300 million tons of the former and 3 billion tons of the latter. The amount of iron mined has risen rapidly in the last decade, from 430,000 tons in 1955 to nearly three times that figure today. While an increasing proportion of these minerals are being used in Mexico's industrialization, sales to the United States still account for over one-fourth of Mexico's export trade. Mexico also has rich petroleum resources. Once the world's major exporter of crude oil, the country's production fell sharply in the years leading up to and following expropriation of foreign oil companies in 1938. Since 1946, the government petroleum company,

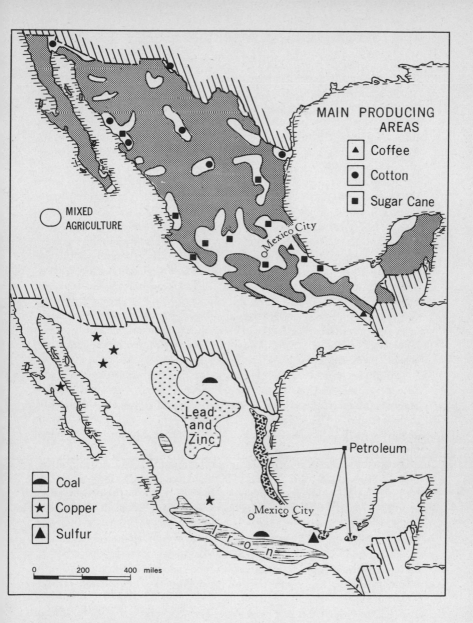

MAIN PRODUCING
AREAS

▲ Coffee

● Cotton

■ Sugar Cane

MIXED
AGRICULTURE

Mexico City

Lead
and
Zinc

Petroleum

● Coal

★ Copper

▲ Sulfur

Mexico City

Iron

0   200   400 miles

Pemex, has raised production to a level second in Latin America only
to Venezuela. Self-sufficient in refining capacity, Mexico is fast moving
into the petrochemical field as well.

16. Industry and Transportation

In recent decades, Mexico has made very substantial progress toward becoming a modern industrial nation. The traditional pattern of economic dependence upon mining and agriculture has been broken. Although over half the labor force are still engaged in agriculture and less than 15 per cent in manufacturing, the latter now contribute slightly more to the gross national product. The original emphasis upon food processing, textiles, and basic consumer goods is rapidly giving way to heavy industry and more complex goods. An iron-and-steel industry, centered near Monterrey, is the largest in Latin America outside Brazil; indeed, it produces roughly one-third the entire region's output of steel. Puebla is one of the hemisphere's major textile centers and Mexico City's thousands of factories turn out a wide variety of consumer goods. With an output of 80,000 vehicles per year, Mexico's automotive industry is proportionately equal to the more populous Brazil. Postwar Mexican administrations have placed a heavy emphasis on the development of power resources. Although Mexico is well endowed with coal and petroleum, which permit steam and diesel generation of electricity, increased attention is being paid to hydroelectric power. The government bought out U.S. and Canadian power companies in 1960 and sharply increased investment in this key sector.

Despite its rugged terrain, Mexico is well on the way to an adequate and integrated transportation system. Although east-west connections and secondary roads are still poor, the main cities are linked by rail, highway, and air. Completion of existing programs will go far toward achieving a network that will knit the republic into an effective national unit.

Most of the country's 15,000 miles of railroads were constructed by foreign firms during the Díaz era. Both roadbeds and rolling stock deteriorated during the years of revolutionary warfare in the countryside, and there was little incentive for further investment by foreign stockholders. Government expropriations and purchases of most lines between 1937 and 1950 paved the way for their modernization and rehabilitation during the past decade. With considerable financial assistance from U.S. and international public lending institutions, a fairly efficient national rail system is now providing essential passenger and freight service.

Highway construction has taken place largely since 1940. From 6,000 miles of roads in that year the total rose to nearly 25,000 in 1960 and has shown a proportional increase since then. The number of buses in use has reached 30,000 and that of trucks has passed 350,000. More

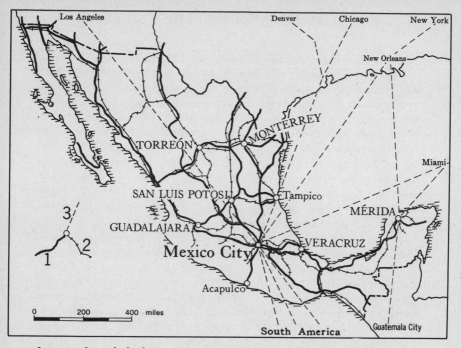

1—main through highway; 2—major railroad; 3—selected international air routes

than 500,000 passenger cars are now in use, a fivefold increase since prewar days. If U.S. tourists are included, there are today nearly a million vehicles on Mexican roads.

In recent years, aviation has become a major element in the Mexican transportation system. With Mexico City as the hub, a network of national lines reaches out to all important cities and main provincial towns. Air travel has brought Mexico into much closer contact with the rest of Latin America and Europe. It has also helped to unite the country. Lacking both seaports and navigable rivers, Mexico has never relied upon inland or coastal waterways for transportation; its growing merchant marine is oriented toward the country's international maritime commerce.

17. The Capital and Political Life

Since its revolution, Mexico has developed a highly centralized governmental system and a broadly representative majority party. The resulting mechanisms for national decision-making are in many respects the most efficient and responsive in Latin America. Almost all important interests in the country are represented in the governmental process. Much power rests in the hands of the President, but his term is limited to a single six-year period. And no President is the stooge of his predecessor. Moreover, the intraparty selection process has consistently come up with able, experienced chief executives, each of whom appears to have been uniquely suited to the needs of his time. Although Mexico is nominally a federal system, real authority is concentrated in the central government in Mexico City.

The key element in the Mexican political-governmental structure is the Institutional Revolutionary Party, or PRI, which has evolved in response to the changing needs of the postrevolutionary nation. Following the fall of strongman Díaz in 1911, the country went through a period of profound political and institutional instability, which included an abortive effort at counterrevolution and civil war among factions that disagreed on how far the revolution should go beyond Francisco Madero's original slogan of "effective suffrage, no re-election." Venustiano Carranza defeated rivals Pancho Villa and Emiliano Zapata, and presided over the promulgation of the famed Mexican Constitution of 1917, which established the legal basis for a sweeping social revolution. When Carranza sought to impose a puppet as his successor in 1920, he was ousted by his chief political-military lieutenants, Alvaro Obregón and Plutarco Elías Calles. As President (1920–24), Obregón began to consolidate the revolution's gains, particularly in the field of education. His assassination in 1928, just after his election to a second term, led to the formation of a political party embracing all major segments that supported the revolution as a means of institutionalizing power.

The National Revolutionary Party (PNR) enabled Calles, who had been President in the period 1924–28, to run the country from behind the scenes until 1935, when he was forced into exile by President Lázaro Cárdenas. Cárdenas transformed the party from a network of regional machines into a truly national organization based on major interest groups: labor, the peasantry, the armed forces, and the "popular" sector, composed chiefly of government employees, white-collar workers, and small businessmen. The organization was renamed the Party of the Mexican Revolution (PRM); the President served as arbiter of conflicts among the country's major internal groups and pushed ahead with the "revived" revolution. Subsequently the military was

Mountain areas are shaded; elevations of selected peaks are given in feet above sea level

dropped as a separate sector and the line between party and government activities was drawn more clearly. In 1945, the party became known as the Institutional Revolutionary Party.

The revolutionary party has manifested considerable flexibility and responsiveness to the demands of such major groups as businessmen, industrialists, and agriculturalists. President Ávila Camacho (1940–46) stressed national unity and moderation; Miguel Alemán, a businessman, emphasized industrialization; Ruíz Cortines (1952–58), a long-time government official, gave continued priority to economic development. Under López Mateos, the government paid somewhat greater attention to the labor situation. Gustavo Díaz Ordaz, elected for the 1964–70 period, follows the general mold of his predecessors, having served during the preceding six years as Minister of Government. In keeping with the trend toward increased democratization, the opposition parties—which have long been permitted to contest elections—have now been guaranteed minority representation.

18.   International Trade and Relations

With its relatively diversified and developed economy, Mexico is one of the leading commercial nations of Latin America. Its major import needs—capital goods, industrial raw materials, and luxury consumer goods—are supplied chiefly by the United States, with Europe furnishing less than 20 per cent. Similarly, its exports of cotton, coffee, metals, sugar, and food products are largely absorbed by the U.S. market. In 1963, Mexican exports to the United States reached $600 million and imports topped $850 million. Mexican purchases abroad have tended to outrun sales. In 1958, Mexico imported goods worth over $1.1 billion while exporting commodities valued at only $700 million.

Although the United States remains Mexico's major trading partner, commerce with Western Europe, Japan, and South American countries has increased in recent years. In the case of Great Britain and West Germany, this represents the re-establishment of pre–World War II patterns; Japan has become a chief importer of Mexican cotton. Since joining the Latin American Free Trade Association, Mexico has been one of its most active and aggressive members, greatly expanding its trade with the South American continent. In 1964, Mexico exported wheat to Communist China, but this may turn out to have been a one-shot operation.

Mexico's "independent" foreign policy is fundamentally a result of the revolution and, particularly, of the difficulties Mexico encountered during the period prior to World War II. Mexicans have a vivid memory of the heavy pressures, including repeated threats of foreign intervention, that were brought to bear on their country during the militant phase of the revolution and that surrounded the oil expropriation of 1938. Hence they place very heavy emphasis on nonintervention and self-determination as cardinal principles of foreign policy. The Mexican position on nonintervention covers not only one state's interference in the internal affairs of another, but also collective action by a group of states or a regional organization. Thus, Mexico has so far refused to accept the validity of the Organization of American States' 1964 decision calling for a mandatory break in diplomatic and economic relations with the Castro regime. Mexico adheres strongly to the right of any people to transform the existing order of their country, even by violent revolution. Remembering that until World War II Mexico's revolutionary regimes were repeatedly denounced as "Communist" by elements in the United States desiring intervention to protect their financial interests, Mexicans have been unwilling to agree to measures against Cuba. Thus, at inter-American meetings they have frequently voted against the U.S. position. Nevertheless, Mexican–U.S. relations have

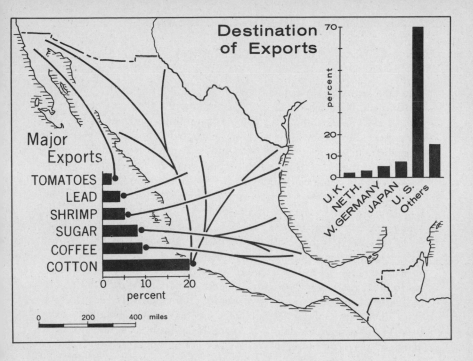

Destination of Exports

Major Exports

- TOMATOES
- LEAD
- SHRIMP
- SUGAR
- COFFEE
- COTTON

0   10   20 percent

0   200   400 miles

percent: U.K. NETH. W.GERMANY JAPAN U.S. Others

been friendly in the postwar period and are growing closer. The Presidents of the two countries have exchanged visits, U.S. Government loans and private investment in Mexico have soared, and a variety of joint development projects have been undertaken.

In recent years, Mexico has also come to play a more active role in world as well as hemispheric affairs. President López Mateos, during his recently completed six years in office, stressed closer links with South American countries and cultivated ties with Western Europe. In international conferences and organizations Mexico has championed peaceful settlement of international disputes and disarmament, particularly limitations on nuclear weapons in Latin America. This diplomatic activity has brought Mexico into closer contact with the Afro-Asian nations. Mexico's world role, combined with its noteworthy successes in the developmental field, has resulted in recognition of the country (together with Brazil) as one of the two most important in Latin America. Mexico's 7 per cent growth in GNP in 1964 and political stability compensate for her smaller size and population in the eyes of many foreign observers.

19. Central America as a Region

The area between Mexico and Colombia remains one of the most agricultural and least urbanized in all Latin America. The vast majority of the 14 million inhabitants of these six republics and one colony are subsistence farmers who raise chiefly corn and beans and live outside or at the margin of the money economy; only a relatively small proportion of the labor force produce the export crops for which the region is noted. Central American cities, in size at least, are on a par with provincial centers in Mexico or most of the South American countries. Guatemala City, with more than 400,000 inhabitants; Panama City, Managua, San Salvador, and San José, with about 300,000 inhabitants each; and Tegucigalpa, with a population of about 150,000, are the only urban centers of any real consequence.

Although some headway toward economic diversification has been made in recent years, the Central American countries are still dangerously dependent upon one or two export commodities. In recent years, over 75 per cent of the exports of Guatemala and Costa Rica have been in coffee and bananas, while for Honduras the figure has been above 60 per cent. Similarly, coffee and cotton have earned El Salvador and Nicaragua four-fifths and three-fifths, respectively, of their foreign exchange. It should be noted, however, that as late as 1957 the corresponding figures for El Salvador and Costa Rica were 90 per cent and for Nicaragua 80 per cent. The region's economic growth has averaged nearly 5 per cent yearly since 1950.

The countries of Central America are often called "banana republics," normally in disparagement. Historically, much of the area's foreign investment, particularly during the early decades of this century, was in banana plantations, and the United Fruit Company engaged in many activities other than growing bananas. Today, bananas are the chief export of only one country, Honduras; they have dropped to 25 per cent of Costa Rica's exports, to less than 20 per cent of Panama's, and to only 8 per cent of Guatemala's. Moreover, there has been a marked tendency, spurred by both plant disease and nationalistic pressures, for "UFCO" to divest itself of its large holdings and to purchase bananas from independent growers.

The five northernmost countries share a common historical experience. A single administrative unit during colonial days, they remained together from independence in 1821 until 1838. Efforts to reconstitute the federation, either by diplomacy or force, continued to the end of the century and established a tradition of intervention in one another's

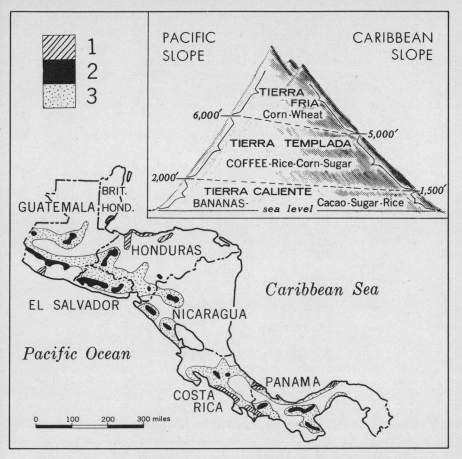

Major areas of production: 1—bananas; 2—coffee; 3—corn and other subsistence crops
Diagram at upper right shows in general terms the vertical zones in Central America

internal political affairs that has carried down to the present. In recent years, the movement for reintegration of Central America has gained momentum, particularly in the economic and cultural fields. An Organization of Central American States (ODECA) came into existence in the 1950's and has been followed by the Central American Common Market (*see Map 59*).

Although these countries do have much in common, there are significant differences that should not be overlooked. Three-fifths of the inhabitants of Guatemala are Indians and only one-twentieth are European; in Costa Rica, the proportions are reversed, with four-fifths European and less than 1 per cent Indian. Honduras, El Salvador, and Nicaragua have overwhelmingly mestizo populations; Nicaragua has more Negroes than Indians. Panama has a very sizable mulatto population, and Negroes outnumber both Europeans and Indians. British Honduras is predominantly Negro. This racial diversity is matched by variations in the political sphere. Costa Rica is often described as the foremost democracy in all Latin America, while Nicaragua and Honduras are among the most politically underdeveloped. But as late as 1944, dictators held sway in the northern four countries, Costa Rican democracy was undermined by a rigged election, and Panama was recovering from a brief but traumatic experience with Arnulfo Arias, a Nazi-admiring authoritarian. It is only in the last two decades that the political paths followed by these countries have markedly diverged.

20. Guatemala, British Honduras, and El Salvador

Guatemala is the most populous of the Central American states, yet, with 4.4 million persons in an area of 42,000 square miles, it is far from overpopulated. By the time of the Spanish conquest in the first half of the sixteenth century, the indigenous inhabitants were concentrated in the volcanic highlands of the southern one-third of the country. Here, at an altitude of almost 5,000 feet, the city of Antigua became the colonial capital of all Central America. By the latter part of the nineteenth century, the large estates in the area had been turned to coffee production. The coastal lowlands were unused until the introduction of banana plantations, first in the east, before World War I, and then, in the mid-1930's, on the Pacific coast.

Since colonial days, political power in Guatemala has rested in the hands of a small number of European landholders. After independence, order was maintained by a series of military dictators, the last of whom, Jorge Ubico, governed for thirteen years before being ousted by a popular uprising in 1944. The country subsequently went through a decade-long social revolution, the most sweeping in the area, but since 1954 it has made relatively less progress in the political and social spheres than have its neighbors. Relations with the United States, which deteriorated during the government of reformist-nationalist Juan José Arévalo (1945–51), reached crisis proportions as President Jacobo Arbenz, in collaboration with the Guatemalan Communist Party, swung the revo-

1—volcano; *2*—highland area (over 1,640 feet above sea level)

lution far to the left. In the face of isolation by its neighbors, a U.S.–supported exile invasion, and the alienation of the armed forces, the Arbenz regime fell in June, 1954.

Colonel Carlos Castillo Armas' efforts to return the country to the "authentic" aims of the 1944 revolution were cut short by an assassin's bullet in mid-1957. After a period of considerable instability, relatively free elections brought General Miguel Ydígoras Fuentes to the Presidency in 1958. His personalism and divide-and-rule tactics helped stall political development, and most civilian groups supported the military coup of March 31, 1963, which placed Colonel Enrique Peralta in control of the government. In 1964, a constituent assembly began work toward a return to constitutional government. During this period Guatemala has enjoyed economic prosperity, but guerrilla elements have been active in some rural areas, and there have been sporadic outbreaks of terrorism in the cities. In most respects, the political development of the country has not progressed in the past fifteen years.

Like its predecessor, the present regime has actively pressed Guatemala's claims to British Honduras (sometimes called Belize), a small colony on the Atlantic coast containing slightly over 100,000 persons, chiefly of Negro descent. In recent years, each British step toward giving the colony self-government has provoked strong Guatemalan reaction. In February, 1965, elections were held in Belize which gave support to George Price and his independence-oriented Peoples United Party. Until it receives satisfaction on the Belize question, Guatemala continues to block admission of Jamaica and Trinidad to the Organization of American States.

With slightly over one-fifth the area of its northern neighbor and a population fast nearing 3 million, El Salvador is the only Central American country yet experiencing a real land shortage. Traditionally, the hold of the few wealthy families—estimated at no more than fifty—controlling the coffee and cotton lands has been among the tightest in Latin America. But this too is changing. Although no Salvadorian "revolution" has run its full course, the net result of several such movements since 1944 has been to weaken the position of the entrenched elite and to broaden the base of the government. A radical leftist coup prospered briefly in late 1960, but moderate reform forces led by Colonel Julio Rivera won out early the next year. Elected constitutional President in 1962, Rivera has since led his nation to substantial, if gradual, progress toward economic development with social justice.

21. Honduras, Nicaragua, and Costa Rica

Slightly larger than Guatemala, but with only half its population, Honduras comes the closest of any Latin American country to being a "banana republic." In colonial days, only the western highlands relatively close to Guatemala and El Salvador were densely settled, but in the past fifty years, and largely due to the efforts of the United Fruit and Standard Fruit companies, the Caribbean coast has become the economic center of the country, and bananas the ranking export.

1—volcano; *2*—highland area (over 1,640 feet above sea level)

General Tiburcio Carías Andino was elected President of Honduras in 1932 and remained in office until 1948, when at the age of seventy-two he gave way to a hand-picked and duly elected successor, Juan Manuel Gálvez. In the 1954 elections, the old *caudillo* failed in a bid for another presidential term. Although the Liberal candidate, Ramón

Villeda Morales, received a sizable plurality, he was not allowed to take office until more than three years later, during most of which time Gálvez's Vice President governed the country until ousted by a military junta. From January, 1958, to October, 1963, Villeda headed a generally progressive and sound administration that helped Honduras to catch up with the twentieth century. Then, only ten days before the scheduled presidential balloting, the Chief of the Armed Forces, Colonel Osvaldo López, seized power. In more than eighteen months López has done little toward returning the country to constitutional normalcy beyond permitting the election of a constituent assembly.

Nicaragua, the largest of the Central American countries (it is seven times the size of El Salvador), is also the most sparsely populated. The great bulk of its fewer than 2 million inhabitants live in the western lowlands, raising corn, cattle, and sugar for internal consumption and cotton for export. Nearby highland areas are planted to coffee. Nicaragua's political life is as underdeveloped as its economy. Political chaos led to U.S. intervention in 1912, and the Marines were not finally withdrawn until 1933. Three years later, Anastasio Somoza, the U.S.– trained and supposedly "apolitical" commander of the National Guard, seized power. For the next two decades he ran the country efficiently and ruthlessly while amassing a huge family fortune. The dictator's assassination in 1956 did not end the dynasty, for his son Luís succeeded to the Presidency. The latter's policy of "controlled liberalization" led to the election of René Schick, a political cohort of the Somozas, as President in 1963. Anastasio Somoza, Jr. (Tachito), who still controls the military, harbors intense presidential aspirations, so Somoza control of Nicaragua seems likely to enter its fourth decade unless opposition forces can show greater vitality and unity than in the past. Schick's efforts to head a constructive administration are hampered by the fact that both Liberal and Conservative party candidates began to campaign actively before the mid-point in his term had been reached.

Only one-third the size of Nicaragua, Costa Rica has a population of just under 1.5 million. Originally colonized by small farmers, who settled in a fertile, volcanic-ash mountain basin in the central highlands, Costa Rica has developed without the large landholding elite common to other Central American countries, and thus enjoys a more democratic society. By 1830, considerably earlier than in other parts of Central America, coffee had become the chief export crop. Exportation of bananas grown on the Caribbean coast began fifty years later, and by 1909 Costa Rica was the world's leading producer; yet by the outbreak of World War II, exports had dropped to almost nothing, owing to plant disease. Subsequently, the United Fruit Company opened new plantations on the Pacific coast, and by the 1950's Costa Rica was again a major exporter.

Costa Rica is the political paragon of the region. Between 1889 and 1917, five successive Presidents completed their terms, as did six others between 1920 and 1944. In 1944, Rafael Calderón Guardia departed from Costa Rican tradition and rigged the elections. Defeated in his bid for a second term in 1948, Calderón, seeking to remain in power by force, formed an alliance with Communist paramilitary forces. José "Pepe" Figueres led the democratic forces to victory after a brief civil war. (The army was subsequently abolished.) In 1953, Figueres was overwhelmingly elected President and headed a liberal reformist administration which repeatedly came into conflict with the Somoza dictatorship. Because of a split in the ranks of Figueres' National Liberation Party, the opposition won narrowly in 1958, but in 1962 Francisco Orlich (Figueres' candidate) won handsomely. Costa Rican democracy appears firmly rooted, but the phenomenal rate of natural population increase—above 4 per cent per year—constitutes a great handicap to the government's developmental program. A volcanic eruption in 1963–64, which covered much of the best farmland near San José with volcanic ash, constituted a major economic disaster for the country.

22. Panama and the Canal

The Republic of Panama owes its existence to the canal which cuts it in two in order to link the Atlantic and Pacific for the benefit of world maritime commerce. The acquisition of California led to a U.S. decision to build a canal. When, in 1903, the Colombian Congress refused to ratify the necessary treaty, the Panamanians revolted and with U.S. support gained nominal independence. The Hay–Bunau-Varilla Treaty granted the United States all power, "as if it were sovereign," in a ten-mile-wide Canal Zone, together with the right to intervene militarily to maintain order in the Republic. Not until this provision was dropped in the 1936 treaty revision did Panama become in fact an independent nation rather than a U.S. protectorate.

After a decade of construction, the Panama Canal was opened to traffic in 1914. Since that time, U.S. payment to the Panamanian Government ($1,930,000 annually, as of today), wages paid to Canal Zone employees, and purchases of foodstuffs and other supplies by the Panama Canal Company amount to over $85 million annually and constitute the most important element of Panama's national income. Banana production, roughly equal to that of Guatemala and Costa Rica, provides the country's major export commodity, followed by frozen shrimp. Realization that the present lock-type canal is obsolescent and will soon need to be replaced with one at sea level has sharpened Panamanian feelings that increased earnings from the Canal are essential to the nation's solvency and development. Combined with the sharp contrast in living standards between the Zone and the Republic, increasing sensitivity on the issue of sovereignty, and racial tensions (more than half the people of Panama are mulatto), this has given rise to repeated anti-U.S. demonstrations, culminating in the "flag riots" of January, 1964.

With a population approaching 1,250,000, Panama is still sparsely populated. Control of national life rests in the hands of an upper-class minority, but a small, growing middle class is beginning to make its weight felt. Panamanian politics have been marked by political instability: when Roberto Chiari took office in 1960, he was Panama's thirty-fourth chief executive in its fifty-seven years of life as a nation, but only its thirteenth constitutionally elected President. Although the accomplishments of the Chiari Administration were limited, its record compared favorably with most of its predecessors. Arnulfo Arias was ousted in 1941 and again in 1951 for his dictatorial ambitions. Colonel José "Chichi" Remón, Commandant of the National Guard (Panama's only military force), and long the major behind-the-scenes political figure, won the 1952 election and gave the country a relatively honest

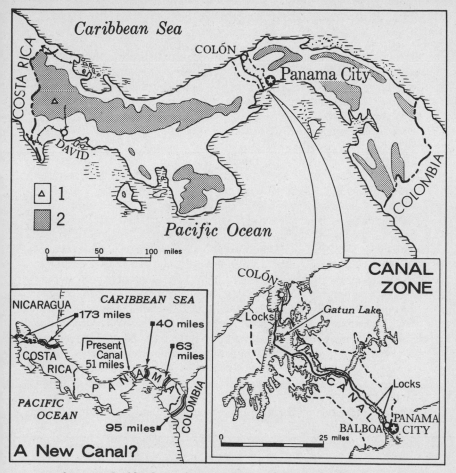

1—volcano; 2—highland area (over 1,640 feet above sea level)

and effective administration until his work was cut short by an assassin's bullets in January, 1955. Ernesto de la Guardia, elected in 1956 as the government's candidate, served out his four-year term and then presided over balloting won by the opposition candidate, Roberto Chiari. In May, 1964, Marco A. Robles, Chiari's Minister of Government, won election to the Presidency. Robles' administration has taken a firmer line with regard to leftist agitation, but it has also initiated overdue reforms and sought an acceptable new treaty covering the construction and operation of a sea-level canal.

23. Peoples of the Caribbean

Racially and culturally, the Caribbean peoples bear little resemblance to their Central American neighbors. While the population of the mainland is predominantly mixed Indian-European, on the islands these elements are numerically insignificant in relation to Negroes and mulattoes. Both the peaceful Arawaks and the warlike Caribs, who populated the Antilles at the time of discovery, were virtually wiped out by battle, disease, and overwork during the first decades of the colonial period. Unlike the indigenous populations of Mexico and the Andean region, they would not reproduce in subjugation. Thus, although there were perhaps 1 million inhabitants on the island of Hispaniola at the beginning of the sixteenth century, all but a few had perished by 1540. At the same time, the number of white colonists in the Caribbean grew relatively slowly as Mexico and Peru came to be the centers of Spanish settlement. But the small number of soldiers, sailors, bureaucrats, planters, indentured servants, freebooters, and transported criminals who did populate the area's isolated military outposts and ports during the first century and a half of the colonial period gave rise to what in the eighteenth century became a small but powerful European elite. As every European power sought a foothold in the Caribbean, the Spanish, French, and British were joined by the Dutch, Danes, and Swedes.

The rise and prosperity of the Europeans rested upon the introduction of sugar cultivation, which also led to the repopulation of the islands by Negro slaves brought over from Africa. Forced out of Brazil by the Portuguese in 1654, the Dutch sugar planters occupied some of the smaller islands of the Lesser Antilles and their agricultural techniques were soon copied by the British and French. After the turn of the century, Haiti and Jamaica developed into the major producers of sugar, molasses, and rum. Sugar prosperity began to ebb in the middle of the nineteenth century as a result of the abolition of slavery and the rapid increase of beet sugar production in Europe. Abolition also led to the arrival of the final major element in the region's complicated ethnic mixture, large numbers of Asiatic field laborers, chiefly from India and the East Indies. As elsewhere in Latin America, small numbers of Syrians, Lebanese, Chinese, and Jews play a significant role in commercial life. The more than 23 million inhabitants of the Caribbean's five independent nations and various autonomous states, colonies, and territories are a distinctive breed, with the proportions varying greatly from one area to another.

Cuba, the region's largest and most populous country with nearly 7.5 million inhabitants, is perhaps 40 per cent Negro; 30 per cent mixed, chiefly mulatto; and 30 per cent of European extraction. Over

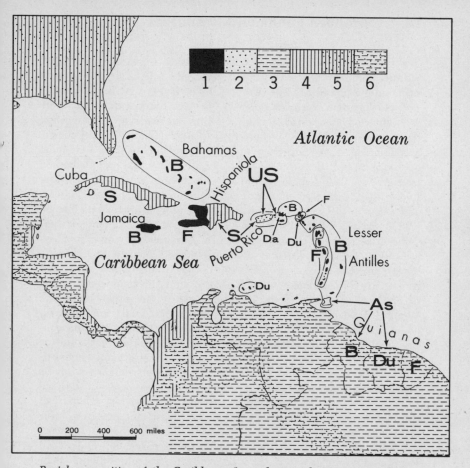

Racial composition of the Caribbean: 1—predominantly Negro; 2—predominantly European; 3—predominantly Indian; 4—mixed, with a large proportion of Negro; 5—mixed Negro and European; 6—mixed Indian and European *Other major cultural influences in the West Indies and Guianas:* US—United States; As—Asiatic (chiefly from India); B—British; Da—Danish; Du—Dutch; F—French; S—Spanish

90 per cent of the more than 4.5 million Haitians are black, and most of the remainder mulatto; at the other end of the island, the Dominican population of over 3.5 million is about 70 per cent mulatto, 15 per cent Negro, and 15 per cent white. On the British islands the whites average only 2 per cent of the total.

24. Caribbean Lands and Resources

The Caribbean islands share a common climate, topography, and agriculture. The core of the Antilles is a massive fold of crystalline rock containing a number of volcanic peaks. The larger islands also contain areas of limestone lowlands emerging from upraised coral reefs. With soils unusually fertile for the tropics, they are capable of supporting quite dense populations. The larger islands—particularly Cuba, Jamaica, and Trinidad—have some basic mineral resources, but the others must get along as best they can on their agricultural output, supplemented by a growing tourist trade. Trinidad, with its petroleum resources, and Puerto Rico, with more than a thousand manufacturing establishments and access to U.S. markets, have attained the highest per capita income —$830 for the latter in 1964—while the erstwhile economic leader, Cuba, has dropped behind since Fidel Castro came to power in January, 1959. Jamaica's economy is prospering—its bauxite and alumina exports bring in more than U.S. $100 million annually, and sugar and rum another $50 million; there is also an annual income from tourism of $50 million. Fruit, cocoa, and bananas are the backbone of the Windward Islands' export trade. Sugar, bauxite, and rice make up about 70 per cent of British Guiana's exports. Surinam exports considerably more bauxite than British Guiana, but is less important as a sugar producer. The Netherlands Antilles enjoy a somewhat artificial prosperity that could be jeopardized if Venezuela carries out its plan to refine its own crude oil.

Sugar is still the leading product of the Caribbean as a whole. Despite successive bad harvests, Cuba remains the ranking exporter of this commodity. More than 60 per cent of Haiti's limited foreign-exchange earnings come from sugar, while for the more diversified Dominican Republic the proportion is still well over 50 per cent. Although their production is comparatively small, the British and French islands are even more dependent upon sugar.

The trade winds have played a most important role in the development of the Caribbean islands. These steady winds from the east facilitated navigation in the centuries during which the sailing ship was the lifeline of the region; they brought the heavy rains that washed alluvial deposits off the mountainsides and carried the fertile soil into the valleys; they still bring the precipitation necessary to raise cash crops such as sugar, cocoa, coffee, and tobacco, as well as needed foodstuffs. The other winds characteristic of the region—hurricanes—are less beneficial. Huge whirlpools of violently moving air sweeping out of the Caribbean toward the United States, they destroy crops and houses and at times devastate entire islands.

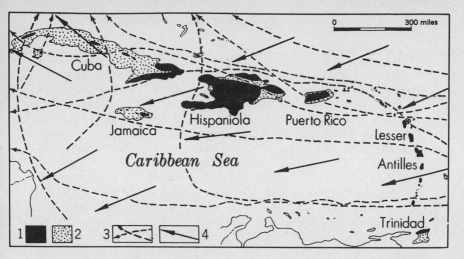

1—crystalline rock area; *2*—sedimentary rock area; *3*—tracks of representative hurricanes which have passed through the West Indies during the past twenty years; *4*—prevailing wind

While the seventeen republics of mainland Latin America all won their independence at approximately the same time (*see Map 10*), the Caribbean region includes countries that have been independent for 160 years, others that have only recently become self-governing, and numerous islands that are still colonies. Moreover, both of the area's oldest republics were reduced to protectorate status at the beginning of the twentieth century. Haiti, which overthrew the French yoke in 1804, was occupied by U.S. Marines from 1915 to 1934. The Dominican Republic was seized by Haiti shortly after it emerged from Spanish rule in 1821, and did not regain its independence until 1844. Again a Spanish colony from 1861 to 1865, it was occupied by the United States in 1916–24. Cuba could not shake off Spanish rule until 1898, began national life with four years of U.S. military government, and was subject to U.S. armed intervention as late as 1934. Jamaica and Trinidad became self-governing members of the British Commonwealth of Nations in 1962. Martinique and Guadeloupe were incorporated as French Overseas Departments in 1946, and eight years later the Netherlands Antilles and Surinam became autonomous states under the Dutch Crown. Puerto Rico, freed from Spain in 1898, was an unincorporated territory of the United States until in 1952 its electorate overwhelmingly chose "commonwealth" status with internal autonomy, a middle road between statehood and full independence.

25.   Cuba: From Colonialism to Communism

With nearly half the land area and one-third the total population of the Antillean region, and a significant degree of industrialization, Cuba has for some decades been considered one of the more important Latin American countries—this despite its relatively short life as a nation. The closeness of its economic and political ties to the United States, particularly its almost total dependence upon the U.S. sugar market, made it seem an unlikely candidate to become the first Communist outpost in the Western Hemisphere. Yet this transition took place with numbing rapidity in 1959–60, bringing in its wake profound implications for the United States and for all of Latin America. In the autumn of 1962, the issue of Soviet missile bases in Cuba brought the world perilously close to the brink of war.

By 1934, when the United States relinquished its right under the Platt Amendment to intervene in Cuba, a number of crippling weaknesses had been institutionalized in the island's national life. Even the more representative regimes were marked by widespread corruption; the United States had become identified in the popular mind with the brutal dictatorship of General Gerardo Machado (1925–33), and U.S. opposition to the nationalist-reformist regime that came to power through the revolution of 1933 was held responsible for the subsequent rise of Fulgencio Batista as the new military strongman; North American investment multiplied until it became a dominant factor; favored treatment for Cuban sugar, while aiding the island's immediate prosperity, discouraged diversification and led to overdependence upon one cash crop. Thus, for a number of reasons, the economic progress of the 1940's and 1950's was not matched by social and political advancement. Although Cuba enjoyed one of the highest per capita incomes in Latin America, the cities, Havana in particular, progressed and prospered much more than did the rural areas, and the issue of income distribution took on increased importance. In addition, the very closeness of Cuba's ties to the United States caused growing resentment among the younger generation of political activists.

The failure of representative democracy in Cuba did much to facilitate the turn to a mass-based authoritarianism and the acceptance of Communist ideology. Batista ruled through a succession of puppet Presidents from 1934 until 1940, when he personally assumed the office. Development without reform characterized these years, and in 1944 his candidate was defeated by Ramón Grau San Martín. During the next eight years, the 1933 revolutionaries showed that they had lost most of their reforming zeal, as under Grau and his successor, Carlos Prío Socarrás, corruption reached a new high. Then Batista seized

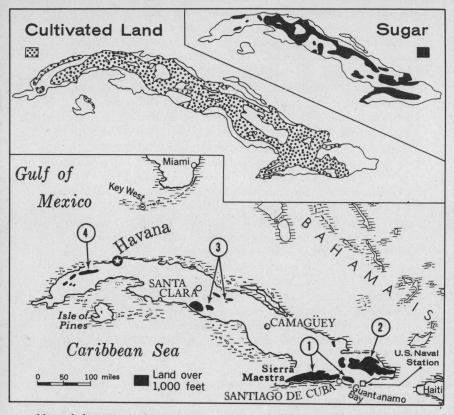

Mineral deposits: 1—chromium, copper, iron, and manganese; *2*—chromium; cobalt, and nickel; *3*—copper, manganese, and petroleum; *4*—copper, iron, and manganese

power through a coup, subsequently holding fraudulent elections. Although economic growth continued (per capita income reached $500 in 1958), the professional and middle classes did not give their support to the dictator and instead aided the armed insurgent movement of Fidel Castro, who pledged himself to a program of political democracy and social justice. As late as 1958, the U.S. Government was identified with the Batista regime, which favored U.S. investment (steadily shifting from sugar to mining and other industry) and cooperated closely with U.S. foreign policy.

By the end of 1958, the indiscriminate terror used by the Batista regime had caused widespread revulsion, Castro had become a popular hero for his ability to hold out in the face of apparently overwhelming military odds, and morale among the armed forces had hit bottom. On January 1, 1959, Batista fled, and Castro came to power determined to initiate a thoroughgoing revolution with a sweeping program of agrarian reform as its touchstone. He quickly enacted measures designed to destroy the economic power base of the landed and commercial upper class and to drastically curb U.S. influence. Following large-scale expropriations of foreign-owned enterprises, more than 90 per cent of all industry came under state control; in the agricultural sphere, the corresponding proportion has reached 70 per cent and is still rising. Between 1958 and 1962, trade with the United States fell from more than $1 billion to a token amount, while that with the Communist bloc rose from an insignificant level to nearly $1 billion. Castro's Cuba increasingly came to resemble an East European "People's Democracy," as local Communists, who had not cooperated with Castro during his fight against Batista, replaced the more moderate leaders of Castro's 26th of July Movement in key positions in the revolutionary government.

The Cuban Communists offered a number of advantages to the relatively inexperienced Castro: an ideological underpinning for the regime and a rationale for its programs; trained and disciplined cadres capable of exercising leadership in a time of rapid and radical change; and an organizational network equipped to mobilize, indoctrinate, and control the broad masses of the population. In addition, alliance with the Communists brought prospects for larger-scale economic and military assistance from the Soviet Union. Knowing that his domestic program and his assistance to revolutionary movements throughout the hemisphere would engender conflict with the United States, Castro actively sought Russian sponsorship and protection. A major trade agreement resulted from the visit of Soviet Deputy Premier Anastas Mikoyan in February, 1960, and the establishment of formal diplomatic relations with the U.S.S.R. and Communist China soon followed. In January, 1961, Cuba broke diplomatic relations with the United States. Following the disastrous failure of the U.S.—supported Bay of Pigs invasion in April, 1961, Castro stepped up the pace of Cuba's conversion into a full member of the Communist bloc. Castro announced the socialist nature of his revolution, began the merger of Fidelistas with long-time Communists in a disciplined Leninist movement, and declared that he himself was a "Marxist-Leninist." He had taken over the leadership of Cuban Communism.

Fully as important, the Soviet Union during 1961 became convinced that long-range maintenance of a Communist state in Latin America was feasible. Their audacious move in seeking to use Cuba as a missile base led to the Kennedy-Khrushchev confrontation in October, 1962, and the withdrawal of the rockets. One result of the Soviet gamble was an increase in Latin American support for the anti-Castro policy of the United States. Thus, in mid-1964, the Organization of American States, from which Cuba's exclusion had been voted at Punta del Este in January, 1962, decided in favor of a collective rupture of diplomatic relations as a sanction against the Castro regime for interventionist activities that included the furnishing of arms to guerrilla groups seeking to overthrow Venezuela's democratic government. Both the United States and the U.S.S.R. appear to share a desire to avoid another showdown over Cuba. Moreover, the problem of Cuban export of revolution appears less critical in the light of a series of encouraging political developments in Venezuela, Brazil, and Chile, as well as improved collective measures for neutralizing Cuban efforts in this field. Yet despite the claims of anti-Castro exile leaders, active resistance on the island remains at a relatively low level. Thus the Cuban problem appears likely to persist for some time in a chronic rather than an acute stage.

Six years after Batista's flight marked the end of the old order, Cuba is a greatly changed country. Its problems and weaknesses are not the same as before, but they are at least equally as serious. Thousands have found new opportunity, but largely because more than 300,000 of the old upper-class, professional, and middle-income population have been driven into exile. New emphasis has been given to mass education, in large part as a vehicle for political indoctrination. The Castro regime has not yet found an answer to the old dilemma of political loyalty versus technical competence in staffing the bureaucracy. While pre-Castro Cuban democracy had grievous flaws, there were at least occasional free elections; since the revolution, not one has been held. Moreover, despite efforts at industrialization and agricultural diversification, Cuba is still as dependent upon sugar as it was before the revolution, and production is considerably lower. The best that can be said is that today the necessities of life are somewhat more equitably distributed among those remaining in Cuba.

26. The Dominican Republic and Haiti

As a legacy from colonial days, the rugged island of Hispaniola is divided into two countries, with French-speaking, densely populated Haiti occupying the western third and the Dominican Republic on the broad eastern plains. The large plantations of Haiti were broken up at independence, and the Negro republic has remained chiefly a land of very small peasant properties; in the Dominican Republic, large estates owned by the white upper-class minority and worked by mulatto laborers are still the common pattern. Extreme rural poverty is the rule in badly overcrowded Haiti, while the Dominican Republic is one of the few areas in the Caribbean in which population pressure is not a major problem, although Santo Domingo is now a city of almost 400,000, and Santiago has 150,000 inhabitants. The largely illiterate Haitian peasant speaks Creole, a patois derived from French and African dialects during colonial days. Literacy in the Dominican Republic is much closer to the Central American average, and Spanish is spoken by nearly all. The less populous but more highly developed Dominican Republic produces four or five times as much sugar as Haiti, and its coffee and cocoa exports each earn more foreign exchange than does Haiti's sugar. Haiti's minor exports of sisal, tobacco, and cocoa bring its total export trade up to only one-fourth that of its neighbor.

Politically as well as economically and socially, Haiti's development has lagged badly. At the time of independence, most Haitians were slaves only recently arrived from Africa; during the 1791–1804 struggle against the French and in the first years of national life most of the white planters and Europeanized mulattoes were killed. During succeeding decades, a small urban elite, largely but not exclusively mulatto, ran the country and profited from public office. Extreme breakdown of public order in 1915 led to U.S. intervention, which lasted until 1934. Resentment by the black middle class of Port-au-Prince (a city of nearly 250,000) over the continued dominance of the lighter-skinned elite triggered the "reformist renovation" administration of President Estimé, but in 1950 a coup re-established the old order under Colonel Paul Magloire. Out of the extreme chaos of 1956–57, Dr. François Duvalier emerged as President. Early in 1964, the tyrannical "Papa Doc," having brutally smashed his opponents, granted himself full power for life. Several small-scale invasions by exiles have so far failed to topple the dictator; meanwhile economic development has come to a standstill in this poorest of all the Latin American countries.

For more than three decades, the history of the Dominican Republic was essentially the history of one man, dictator Rafael Trujillo, who held absolute power from 1930 until his assassination in 1961. While

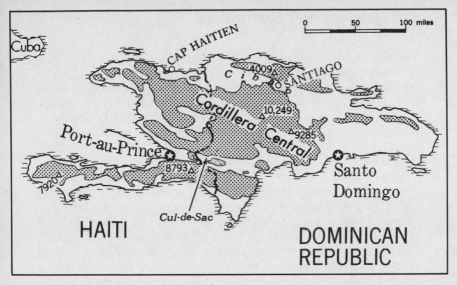

Areas above 1,000 feet are stippled

preserving the traditional social structure in rural areas, Trujillo brought a considerable measure of economic development to the cities. The price of these material benefits was loss of political freedom (and in many cases of life as well) for opponents of the regime and concentration of wealth and power in the hands of the Trujillo clan. Following the dictator's death and an unsuccessful effort by his family and associates to hold on to power, the Dominican Republic experimented with several types of government while striving to establish some form of an effective, representative political system. Reform-minded but administratively inexperienced Juan Bosch was overwhelmingly elected President in December, 1962. Ten months later, he was ousted by a military coup backed by conservative forces. The composition of the governing junta underwent considerable turnover during its year and a half in office, and the military and civilian elite continued to maneuver for power. In April, 1965, a popularly supported coup overthrew Donald Reid Cabral shortly after he made clear his intentions to continue in power through elections scheduled for the autumn. A prolonged period of civil strife ensued, leading to armed intervention by U.S. Marines and airborne troops. This caused a major crisis within the inter-American system.

27. Jamaica and Puerto Rico

The two islands flanking Hispaniola have much in common. Both produce sugar and rum, both have established a profitable tourist trade; both are industrializing and enjoy a relatively high standard of living for tropical areas. In addition, both of these countries have attained substantial independence while retaining a favored relationship with the former colonial power. Jamaica achieved dominion status in 1962; Puerto Rico became a "free associated state" a decade earlier. Each relieves population pressures through emigration to the metropolis.

Jamaica is the larger and more rugged of the two islands. Kingston, which with its immediate environs contains nearly 350,000 of the country's 1,725,000 inhabitants, is the center of manufacturing and commerce. The Jamaicans are overwhelmingly Negro and mulatto. Political life is no longer dominated by the small European element. Indeed, during the past three decades Jamaica has made significant progress toward becoming a parliamentary democracy with a flourishing two-party system. In 1938, Norman Manley, an outstanding lawyer, founded the Peoples' National Party (PNP), which won increased self-government from Great Britain in 1943. In the subsequent elections, however, the Jamaican Labor Party (JLP) of colorful Alexander Busta-mante triumphed. In 1955, the PNP forged ahead, but on the eve of full independence in 1962 the JLP won a close election and the aging Bustamante once again became Prime Minister.

Puerto Rico has developed even more rapidly than Jamaica in recent decades, despite its lack of mineral resources. The reason lies chiefly in the peculiar advantages Puerto Rico has enjoyed as a supplier for thee U.S. market and in the quality of its local political leadership. Despite significant accomplishments in the field of public works and sanitation while a U.S. territory, the people remained poor and the population multiplied rapidly. During the depression, Luis Muñoz Marín organized the Popular Democratic Party, which in 1940 gained control of the territorial legislature. A program of land redistribution coupled with agricultural improvement was inaugurated. Industry was attracted through tax exemptions and low labor costs. With no federal taxes and no customs duties on exports to the mainland, hundreds of light and medium manufacturing plants were erected on the island by U.S. capital. "Operation Bootstrap" led to an almost 500 per cent rise in per capita income over the past twenty-five years, enabling Muñoz Marín to win election after election. In January, 1965, Muñoz stepped down in favor of his carefully groomed successor, Roberto Sánchez Vilella. The marked increase in tourism since Havana became off-limits for free-spending U.S. vacationers has given an additional boost to Puerto

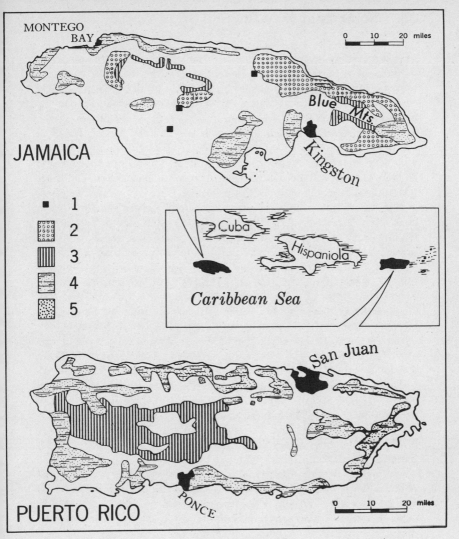

1—bauxite (Jamaica); 2—bananas (Jamaica); 3—coffee; 4—sugar cane; 5—pine-apples (Puerto Rico)

Rico's prosperity. Over 550,000 visitors yearly spend close to $100 million, and U.S. direct capital investment continues at $250 million annually. Population has risen to more than 2.5 million; San Juan is a city of almost 500,000.

28.   Some Islands in the Sun

The West Indies comprise a number of small islands of little economic or political importance, but of increasing interest to North American tourists. Most of these islands boast of mild, breezy weather, bright sun, and sandy beaches. Just north of Cuba and Hispaniola are the approximately 3,000 low-lying coral isles of the Bahamas, a British colony with about 130,000 inhabitants, predominantly Negro. The chief source of income is provided by the several hundred thousand tourists who visit the winter resorts centered around Nassau, a city of nearly 50,000. The sparsely populated Cayman, Caicos, and Turks islands are geographically an extension of the Bahamas.

The U.S. Virgin Islands, an unincorporated territory since their purchase from Denmark in 1917, are a series of small mountain tops protruding from the sea east of Puerto Rico. St. Croix, the largest, has fewer than 15,000 inhabitants and St. John fewer than 1,000. St. Thomas, with its protected harbor of Charlotte Amalie, has a population of over 15,000. Once an important coaling station, St. Thomas is now the center of a small bay-rum industry using alcohol from St. Croix and bay leaves from St. John. Its major function, however, is increasingly that of a thriving tourist center. The British Virgin Islands —which have an area one-half that of the U.S. islands and a population of under 10,000—are also economic satellites of St. Thomas. Indeed, the dollar rather than the pound is the currency commonly in use.

The Netherlands Antilles are composed of three islands off the coast of Venezuela—Curaçao, Aruba, and Bonaire—and three small specks of land 400 miles away (near the British islands of the Lesser Antilles), St. Martin, St. Eustatius, and Saba. Like Surinam (*see Map 30*), they constitute an autonomous state in the kingdom of the Netherlands. Of the total population of about 230,000, nearly 150,000 live in Curaçao, whose capital, Willemstad (65,000 inhabitants), is the commercial and political center of the islands. Nearly 70,000 others live on Aruba. Economic life centers around the large refineries on these two islands, which handle much of Venezuela's crude oil. Tourism, sparked by free-port prices on European imports, is also on the rise.

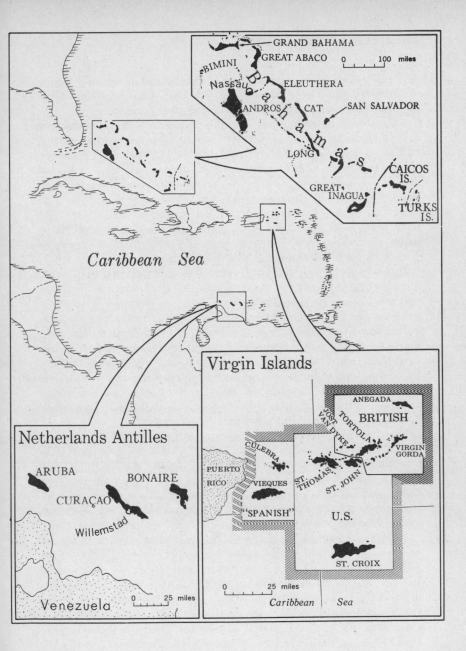

GRAND BAHAMA
GREAT ABACO
0   100 miles
BIMINI
Nassau
B a h a m a s
ELEUTHERA
ANDROS
CAT
SAN SALVADOR
LONG
CAICOS IS.
GREAT INAGUA
TURKS IS.

Caribbean Sea

Virgin Islands

Netherlands Antilles

ARUBA
BONAIRE
CURAÇAO
Willemstad

Venezuela

0   25 miles

PUERTO RICO
CULEBRA
VIEQUES
'SPANISH'

ANEGADA
BRITISH
JOST VAN DYKE
TORTOLA
VIRGIN GORDA
ST. THOMAS
ST. JOHN

U.S.

ST. CROIX

0   25 miles
Caribbean   Sea

29. The Lesser Antilles

A dozen major islands and hundreds of smaller islets create a 500-mile arc between the Virgin Islands and Trinidad. Known as the Lesser Antilles, they are primarily British and French possessions.

Largest and most populous are the French islands of Martinique and Guadeloupe, which have been since 1946 overseas Departments of France. Martinique, with a population of 310,000 and a protected harbor at Fort-de-France, subsists chiefly from production of alcohol and rum, as well as sugar, which is accorded preferential treatment in the French market. Bananas are also exported to France on a large scale. Guadeloupe and its five dependent islands, of which Marie Galante is the most important, has a population equal to that of Martinique. Emigration to France has eased the problem of demographic growth. Sugar and bananas are the islands' chief exports.

Barbados is the only one of the British islands to match the French Departments in population, if not in size. About one-third of the 250,-000 inhabitants dwell in Bridgetown; most of the rural labor force work on the sugar plantations, at least during the harvest months. Urban employment is increasing, chiefly as a result of the growing tourist trade. Without this source of income and preferential treatment in Britain for its sugar, the 166-square-mile island would be hard pressed to support its dense population even at subsistence level. The Windward Islands—Grenada, St. Vincent, St. Lucia, and Dominica—are also overpopulated, placing a great burden on agrarian economies. The total population of the Windwards is about 400,000.

The Leeward Islands of Montserrat, Antigua, St. Kitts–Nevis, and their smaller dependencies, appear incapable of supporting their 160,-000 inhabitants above a mere subsistence level. Like Barbados, Antigua and St. Kitts export sugar, molasses, and rum; similarly, they have benefited from the region's development as a vacation land for free-spending North Americans. Montserrat and Nevis rely upon cotton and bananas.

Federation was long considered the answer to the development problems of the British Caribbean territories, but the federal union broke apart three years after its formation in 1958, as Trinidad and Jamaica showed themselves unwilling to sacrifice their relative prosperity to aid in the development of the lesser islands. In October, 1964, the "Little Seven" decided to go ahead with a more limited federation. Only with continued substantial British assistance can Barbados, the Windwards, and the Leewards become a viable economic entity capable of assuming the responsibilities of political independence.

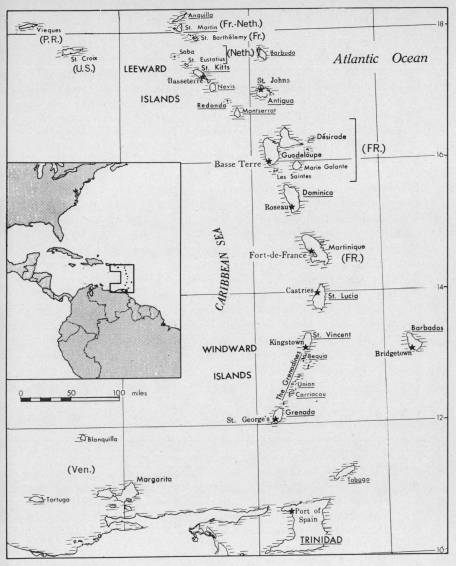

British islands are underlined

30. Trinidad and the Guianas

Located just off the coast of Venezuela, Trinidad has supplemented its own petroleum-based prosperity by refining significant quantities of its neighbor's crude oil. Sugar exports have taken a back seat to industrialization during recent decades. Port of Spain has grown into a bustling city of nearly 150,000, and the U.S. naval and air base at Chaguaramas Bay provides an additional source of income for the nearly 1 million inhabitants of the islands. Political life in Trinidad and Tobago, a small and sparsely populated island neighbor, has a significant racial basis. The Peoples' National Movement of Premier Eric Williams, which has been in power since the elections of 1956, is supported by most of the 45 per cent of the population of African descent, while the Democratic Labor Party draws chiefly from the East Indian 35 per cent. Thus in the 1961 elections the former received 185,000 votes to the latter's 130,000. In nearly a decade in office, Williams has implemented a fairly successful development program.

Although not yet fully independent, British Guiana has been much in the news recently. The proportion of Africans and East Indians is the reverse of that in Trinidad, and race plays a much greater part in political affairs. The East Indians, brought in as plantation labor after the emancipation of Negro slaves in 1838, were until 1947 disenfranchised by strict property and literacy requirements. In 1953, universal suffrage gave victory to the militantly leftist Peoples' Progressive Party (PPP) of Cheddi Jagan, a U.S.–educated dentist. Within a few months, the British, fearing Jagan's marked sympathy for the Communist world, found it necessary to suspend the constitution. After L. Forbes Burnham, once a Jagan lieutenant, took most of the African population into his Peoples' National Congress, new elections were held in 1957. The PPP once more won a sweeping victory, and in 1961 gained 20 of 35 seats with only 43 per cent of the total vote. As rioting and racial clashes continued, the British once more postponed the granting of independence and scheduled elections for December, 1964, to be held under a system of proportional representation. As expected, this action enabled a coalition regime of the PNC and Peter D'Aguiar's conservative United Force to take office.

Roughly one-fourth of British Guiana's 660,000 inhabitants live in Georgetown, the only city of any real importance, and most of the rest live in the coastal belt. Surinam's capital, Paramaribo, contains more than one-third of the total population of about 375,000 (over half Asiatic and only 14 per cent Negro). Since 1950, Surinam has been an autonomous, self-governing part of the kingdom of the Netherlands.

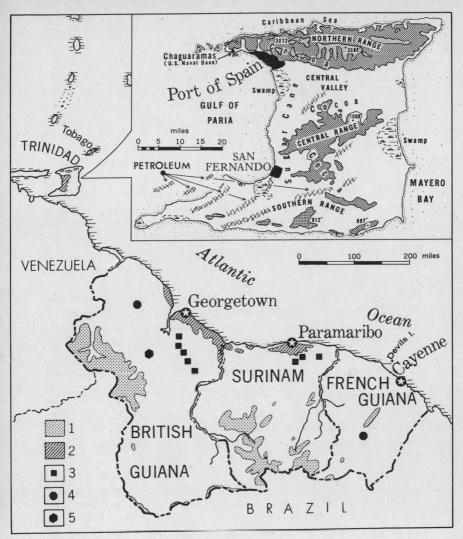

1—highlands over 1,640 feet; *2*—rice and sugar-growing area; *3*—bauxite; *4*—gold; *5*—diamonds

French Guiana, with only 35,000 inhabitants, is of little significance compared to any of its neighbors, but has been awarded the status of a Department of France. Its capital, Cayenne, is a provincial town with a population of 15,000.

THE ANDEAN COUNTRIES

31. The Andes

For six of the South American republics—Venezuela, Colombia, Ecuador, Peru, Bolivia, and Chile—the Andes mountains constitute the most important geographical fact of life. Indeed, the greater part of their 56 million people live in the valleys and basins or on the slopes of the several cordilleras which form the backbone of the continent. And it is this massive continuous barrier, stretching over 4,000 miles, that separates the countries facing the Pacific Ocean from their Atlantic-oriented neighbors. (Although 200,000 square miles of Argentina are covered by the Andes, population and economic life are centered far to the east.) Second only to the Himalayas in height and ruggedness, the Andes can be crossed by rail or coach only at a few widely separated points. A number of peaks reach 20,000 feet, with Mt. Aconcagua on the Chilean-Argentine frontier towering to 22,834 feet, the highest point in the Western Hemisphere. Few passes are lower than 10–12,000 feet, and the width of the parallel ranges is generally at least 200 miles. It is little wonder that transportation is a major bottleneck to development, that regionalism is an important political problem, and that there is relatively little trade even between neighboring nations.

The mineral resources of the Andes, particularly gold and silver, were the chief interest of the Spanish conquerors of the sixteenth century. Mining is still important today in the Andes, but it is chiefly the copper, lead, and tin of Chile, Bolivia, and Peru and the oil of Venezuela that have attracted foreign investors in the past hundred years. Most of the railroads built in the late 1800's, and even after the turn of the century, were designed to facilitate exploitation of these mineral resources. Only in recent years, with the growth of population pressures, have roads been built to open up the trans-Andean plains.

Although the six Andean countries have much in common, the natural unity of the region is far from complete, and there are very significant sociopolitical differences. Ecuador, Peru, and Bolivia (the old Inca Empire) have large unassimilated Indian populations. Venezuela and Colombia are mestizo countries, while Chile's population is essentially European. Most of Venezuela's territory lies outside the Andes; it borders on the Caribbean and the Atlantic, not the Pacific. Chile, on the other hand, falls almost entirely within the Andes.

In the political sphere, an evening-out process appears to be underway. Chile and Colombia have traditionally been considered two of the most stable and democratic of the Latin American republics, and in

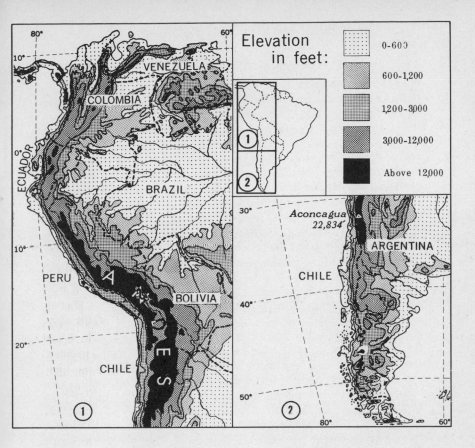

Elevation in feet:
0-600
600-1,200
1,200-3,000
3,000-12,000
Above 12,000

many respects they still merit this distinction. Yet in the postwar period the latter has been plagued by widespread violence, which led to a rather harsh dictatorship in the mid-1950's, while in the former a Communist-led coalition came very close to achieving control of the national government through free elections in 1958 and polled nearly 1 million votes in September, 1964. Historically the most politically retarded, Bolivia is the only one of the six countries thus far to have gone through a sweeping sociopolitical revolution. Venezuela, long a stronghold of dictatorship, has since 1958 enjoyed what is perhaps the most progressive democratic government on the continent. Ecuador, which made encouraging progress toward workable representative government during the 1948–60 period, subsequently ran into stormy political seas and is now the only one of these countries under military rule.

32. Venezuela: History and Politics

Although less than one-fifth of Venezuela is covered by the northeastern arm of the Andes, it is in the basins and slopes of these highlands that most Venezuelans live. The European 20 per cent of the population is concentrated in the cities, together with a portion of the mestizos who make up the bulk of the Venezuelan people. To the southeast of the Andes lies the vast Llanos, a low, level plain stretching from eastern Colombia to the Atlantic and used only for extensive grazing. South of the Orinoco River, the uninhabited Guiana highlands cover nearly half of Venezuela's more than 350,000 square miles. In recent years, the Bethlehem and United States Steel companies have begun to exploit the very large deposits of iron ore on the fringe of the highlands, shipping it down the Orinoco to the sea. In 1964, such exports earned $100 million—25 per cent more than in the preceding year. Venezuelan plans call for the development of a major industrial complex and the construction of a large modern city on the river as a bold step toward incorporating this region into the productive area of the nation. A steel plant is already functioning there.

No country of Latin America has changed as rapidly in the past several decades as oil-rich Venezuela. Prior to World War II, Venezuela was the stereotype of a poor agricultural country run by military strongmen for the benefit of landed oligarchs and at the expense of the downtrodden peasantry. During the first century of its life as a nation, four dictators—José Antonio Páez, Antonio Guzmán Blanco, Cipriano Castro, and Juan Vicente Gómez—held sway for a total of more than seventy years. The building of a modern nation began under Gómez who, upon coming to power in 1908, gradually extended the authority of the central government over areas previously dominated by local *caudillos*. During the 1920's, Venezuela rose rapidly to a position as the world's second largest producer of crude petroleum. With oil as the catalyst, industrialization and urbanization got under way.

After Gómez's death in 1935, the processes of change were felt more directly. The new business and managerial elite made good their claim to a share of social and political leadership while middle and urban working classes grew both in size and restlessness. In 1946, the latter tasted political power when the reformist-revolutionary Democratic Action Party (AD) gained control of the government; but in 1948, it was ousted by a military coup. General Marcos Pérez Jiménez emerged as dictator and squandered the nation's resources until January, 1958, when the military joined in ousting him.

The democratic reform government of President Rómulo Betancourt of the AD (in coalition with the Christian Democrats) brought Vene-

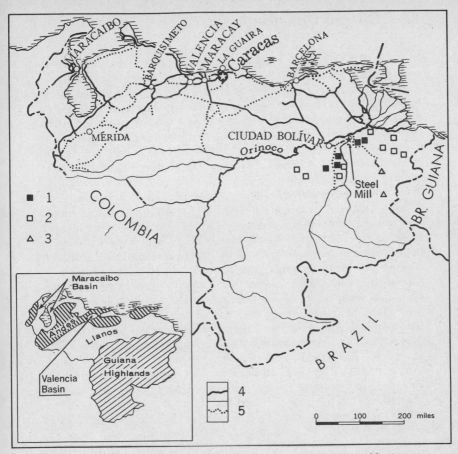

1—iron-ore deposit, worked; 2—iron ore deposit, unworked; 3—gold; 4—main road, paved; 5—main road, gravel

Inset map shows major physical areas

zuela through what can in justice be termed a political, social, and economic revolution during the 1959–64 period. Firmly backed by organized labor and the peasantry, which had benefited from his emphasis on education, housing, and agrarian reform, Betancourt successfully withstood repeated Castro-Communist subversive efforts. During its first year and a half in office, the government of President Raúl Leoni, also of the AD, has continued the constructive work of its predecessor. Nonetheless, guerrilla warfare has persisted.

33. Oil and Urbanization

In terms of its per capita gross national product of nearly $900, Venezuela is the richest and economically most developed country in Latin America. But this high income is still very unevenly distributed and is in part offset by the very high cost of living. Moreover, it is based heavily upon petroleum production for export, a most uncertain foundation for the country's continued prosperity, particularly in light of the world over-supply of oil. No less than 86 per cent of the $5 billion of foreign investment in Venezuela is in oil. More than 90 per cent of the country's export earnings come from this one source, which also provides the government with almost 70 per cent of its revenues. Since 1958, government policies have increasingly taken these considerations into account; the high oil revenues have been used to bring about a more balanced economic development which will leave the country better prepared to live on reduced petroleum earnings. This realism is due not only to the uncertain state of the world oil market, but also to the fact that with only 7 per cent of the world's proven reserves, Venezuela's oil resources could eventually be exhausted by continued high production. Moreover, Venezuela's rate of population growth is one of the highest in the world (more than 3.5 per cent per year); there are over 8.6 million Venezuelan mouths to be fed today, and there will be at least 300,000 more by next year.

Venezuela's oil is exploited chiefly by foreign companies which divide the proceeds with the government. When concessions were first granted, around the time of World War I, the Venezuelan share of the profits was generally about 10 per cent. In 1943, this was raised to a 50-50 basis (with the government portion comprising both taxes and royalties), and under the Betancourt administration the Venezuelan cut rose to at least 60 per cent. The largest of the companies involved is Creole Petroleum, a subsidiary of Standard Oil of New Jersey, followed by Royal Dutch Shell. Creole refines part of its crude oil within the country, but most of Venezuela's production goes to refineries in Curaçao, Aruba, or Trinidad. In recent years, considerable support has developed for proposals that the government require that more of the processing be done in Venezuela; at present, only 2–3 per cent of the Venezuelan labor force is employed in the oil industry.

The great producing fields of Venezuela are located around and under Lake Maracaibo, in the hot, humid western portion of the country. The city of Maracaibo has grown with the oil industry and now numbers 500,000 inhabitants. But the chief beneficiary has been the capital. A city of 200,000 in 1940, Caracas has since grown to nearly 1.5 million persons. The vast public-works projects of Pérez Jiménez in the

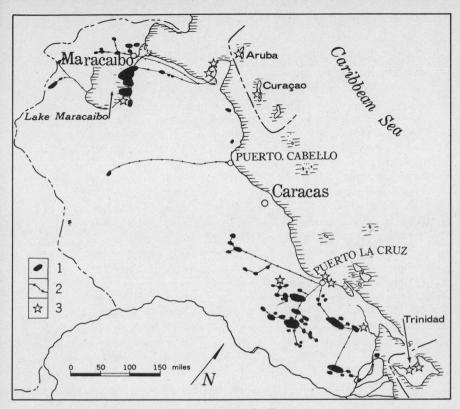

1—petroleum deposit; 2—oil pipeline; 3—oil refinery

decade 1948–58 have made it one of the most modern cities in Latin America. The commercial and industrial as well as the political and cultural center of the nation, it is located in a valley in the Andean highlands, 3,000 feet above its port of La Guaira. In Caracas are found the businessmen, professional people, white-collar employees, and skilled laborers who have benefited the most from the development of the country through the process of "sowing the petroleum." Here also can be found the spreading slums where live the thousands who have flocked to the metropolis in search of a better life and have so far been disappointed in their hopes. Barquisimeto, Valencia, and Maracay (all in the 150,000–200,000 population range), are smaller versions of the capital.

34. Colombia: History and Politics

Perhaps nowhere else in Latin America has geography created greater barriers to the development of a unified nation than in Colombia. Three giant fingers of the Andes reach up from the south, dividing the country into diverse regions and imposing formidable barriers to transportation and communication. The eastern half of the country is as yet largely unsettled and there are other isolated enclaves not effectively incorporated into the nation. Nevertheless, Colombia, with its rapidly growing population of 17 million, is steadily developing into one of the more modern Latin American states.

The area that is now the heart of Colombia was first colonized by Spaniards pushing down the river valleys from the Caribbean coast and up from Ecuador. The Chibcha civilization which they encountered lagged somewhat behind those of the Aztecs, Mayas, and Incas. Gold and emerald mining became the backbone of the economy in the central region, while on the Caribbean coast, planters brought in Negro slaves. Today, about one-half the population is mestizo, one-fifth European, one-fifth mulatto, and the remainder Indian and Negro. Unfortunately the economy is not yet so diversified and the society remains quite stratified, but increasing industrialization is bringing with it a rising degree of social mobility. Coffee, grown chiefly on small farms, provides about 80 per cent of the country's foreign-exchange earnings.

Throughout the interwar period, Colombia was generally considered one of the leading democracies of Latin America, largely because of the absence of the personalist dictators who dominated the scene in so many other countries. Competition between the traditionally dominant Conservative and Liberal parties has always been bitter, yet the Conservatives had peacefully yielded power to the Liberals following the 1930 elections and significant reforms had been enacted during the administrations of President Alfonso López (1934–38 and 1942–45). Following the assassination of the popular Liberal leader Jorge Gaitán, in 1948, violence flared up in large sections of the country. There was general relief when the military took over in 1953, but the regime of General Gustavo Rojas Pinilla forfeited public support when it degenerated into a personalist dictatorship.

The leaders of the traditional parties agreed to cooperate in overthrowing the dictatorship and re-establishing democratic political forms. Since the ouster of Rojas in 1957, all public offices have been shared equally by the Liberals and Conservatives, with the Presidency alternating between the two parties. Under both Liberal President Alberto Lleras Camargo (1958–62) and Conservative Guillermo León Valenica (elected in 1962 for a four-year term), the majority factions of

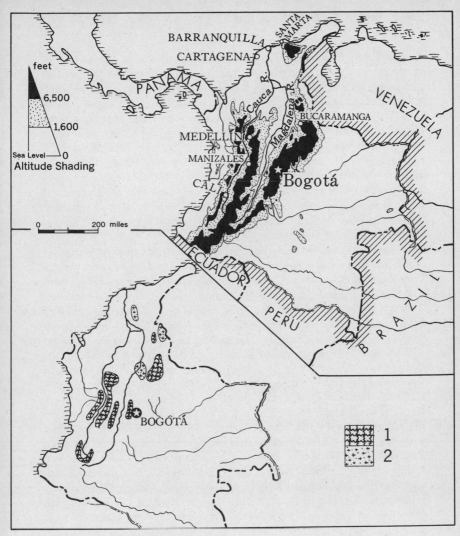

1—coffee; 2—petroleum
Upper map shows major cities and relief features

both parties have supported the National Front government. This system has come under increasing criticism because the two parties are largely upper-class–controlled and have failed to institute reforms.

35. Some Colombian Centers

Colombia provides one of the most graphic examples of the process of urbanization that is changing the face of Latin America. Twenty-five years ago, two-thirds of all Colombians lived on farms or in small towns. Today, nearly half live in cities. In addition to Bogotá, which is one of the ten great metropolises of Latin America, there are three other Colombian urban centers that have passed the half-million mark, while eight more cities each have more than 150,000 inhabitants. The modernizing heartland of Colombia lies within the triangle formed by Bogotá, Medellín, and Cali. Bogotá lies some 8,700 feet above sea level in a sizable basin in the Cordillera Oriental. The seat of government and a major commercial center, this metropolis of 1,500,000 people is often called the "Athens of America," and it still retains cultural pre-eminence within the Andean countries.

Medellín, capital of the department (state) of Antioquia, is located at 5,100 feet in a small basin in the Cordillera Central. Widely known for their enterprise and shrewd business sense, the Antioqueños colonized much of the central triangle of Colombia. Today a city of about 800,-000, Medellín may well be the most important manufacturing center between São Paulo and Mexico City. It is particularly famed for its textiles. In addition, it remains the hub of Colombia's coffee industry.

The most overpopulated Colombian city is Cali, monarch of the Cauca River Valley. In one generation, Cali, nestled at 3,200 feet at the foot of the Cordillera Occidental, has grown from a sleepy provincial town into a city of more than 800,000 inhabitants. Although industry has developed rapidly in recent years, employment opportunities have not caught up with the human influx, which includes many refugees from the violence and banditry that until very recently were rampant in areas to the north and east of the department of Valle. The rich farmlands of the Cauca Valley have traditionally been underutilized, and they are still devoted largely to cultivation of sugar cane and extensive grazing. Hopes for the fuller development of the region's rich potential are largely tied up with the Cauca Valley Corporation (CVC), a multipurpose development agency modeled on the Tennessee Valley Authority. Buenaventura, Cali's port, is rapidly increasing in importance, and Palmira, situated less than twenty miles across the valley from Cali, has grown to over 170,000.

The fourth city of Colombia is the port of Barranquilla near the mouth of the Magdalena River, Colombia's main waterway. With a population of some 500,000, it too is developing into a major industrial center. Barranquilla's growth has continued despite the fact that im-

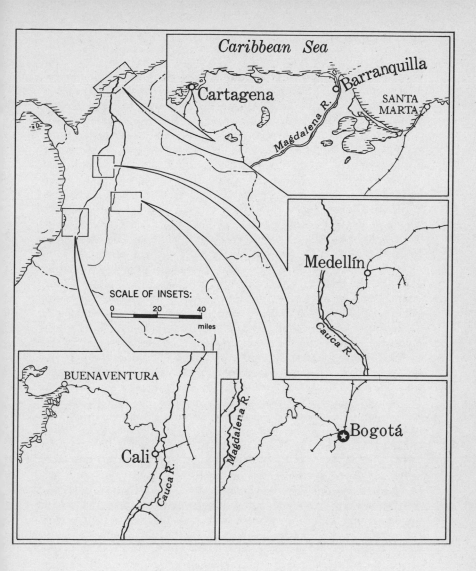

proved road and rail connections have given Cartagena (population 200,000) more of Medellín's export and import traffic. Bucaramanga (250,000) and Manizales (190,000) are important oil and coffee centers.

36. Ecuador

Ecuador is unfortunate in possessing most of the problems of her Andean neighbors while lacking their mineral resources. Half Indian, but still dominated by the "white" tenth of its population, and heavily dependent upon the production of bananas, coffee, and cocoa for export earnings, Ecuador in many respects resembles Guatemala. Its exaggerated regionalism, however, sets it apart. Although the greater proportion of the country's population of over 5 million is concentrated in a series of basins within the Andes, the relatively narrow coastal lowlands have developed into the nation's economic and commercial heartland. Concomitantly, the rapidly growing port of Guayaquil with well over 500,000 inhabitants has come to overshadow Quito, a city of some 300,000 situated at an altitude of 9,300 feet. The often bitter rivalry between the capital—which represents the traditionally conservative, Indian-populated highlands—and the more progressive coastal belt with its chiefly mestizo inhabitants makes Ecuador one of the most difficult of all Latin American countries to govern. The sierra (highlands) area, which includes Quito, contributes almost nothing to the country's foreign commerce and very little to its limited industrial production. Cocoa was the dominant export crop until World War II; by 1957, bananas accounted for over half of all export earnings and they now account for more than 60 per cent. Coffee and cocoa contribute another 20–30 per cent of the country's exports.

Political change in Ecuador has been sporadic. No effective modern party has risen to challenge the traditional Conservatives and Liberals. Nor has the personalist leader provided the vehicle for political development. Four-time President José María Velasco Ibarra (1934–35, 1944–47, 1952–56, and 1960–61) was able to serve out his term only once, and then largely because of the foundation of prosperity, stability, and democracy inherited from his predecessor Galo Plaza (1948–52). Conservative President Camilo Ponce (1956–60) gave Ecuador an unprecedented third successive constitutional administration, but when the aging Velasco took over once again in 1960 affairs rapidly deteriorated. In an atmosphere of popular discontent he was ousted by the armed forces in November, 1961. Although his successor, Carlos Arosemena, showed some promise of being the constructive reformer the situation demanded, his alcoholism led to his replacement in July, 1963, by a military junta. The Ecuadorian people acquiesced in the cancellation of the scheduled 1964 elections and appeared willing to give the fairly progressive-appearing military leaders a chance to cope with the country's problems. By Ecuadorian standards, at least, the junta's first year in power was a constructive one. Its subsequent per-

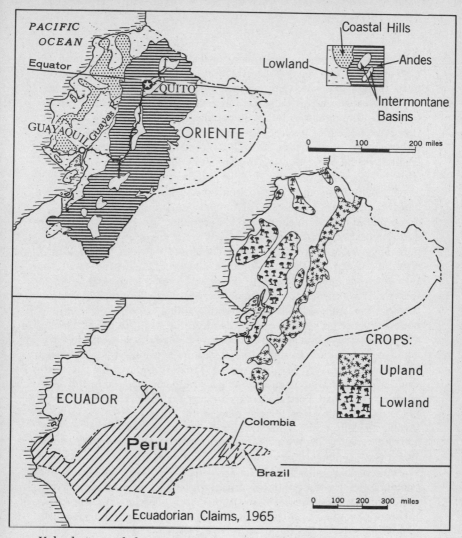

Upland crops include corn and other cereals, sugar cane, and coffee; lowland crops include bananas, coconuts, cocoa, and rice

formance has been somewhat disappointing, and misgivings have been expressed concerning its failure to take steps toward a return to constitutional government.

37. Peru

One of the larger and most populous of the countries of Latin America, Peru was long the region's heartland. For three centuries, from conquest to independence, Lima was the continent's premier city. Today, with approximately 1.6 million inhabitants, Lima ranks with Caracas, Bogotá, and Santiago in terms of population and commerce. Its port, Callao, and Arequipa, well to the south, are both over 150,000 but the great majority of the nearly 12 million Peruvians remain rural dwellers. Nearly half the population are Indians and another 35 per cent mestizo, with the proportions varying sharply in different regions.

Regionalism is even more pronounced in Peru than in Ecuador. The narrow arid coastal strip cut by numerous Andean streams plays a major role in the relatively diversified economic life of the nation. The northernmost of these oases produce cotton, Peru's second leading export. Sugar cane is grown on large plantations outside Trujillo, Peru's fifth-ranking city (75,000 inhabitants), and production nearly matches that of the Dominican Republic. Food crops are grown near Lima to feed the city's teeming population. Nevertheless, Peru is a heavy importer of foodstuffs. Farther to the south, grazing takes on increased importance. Since only a few roads reach from the coast to the highlands, this vast, heavily populated area is devoted chiefly to subsistence farming. Its contribution to the national economy comes from its varied mineral resources (*see Map 39*). In 1963, Peru displaced Japan as the world's leading fishing country, and a 25 per cent increase in fish-meal production pushed Peru's export earnings for 1964 to $667 million.

During the latter part of the nineteenth century, Peruvian politics revolved chiefly around the struggle for power between the "civilist" and "militarist" segments of the entrenched elite. Not until after World War I did a political movement with middle-class leadership emerge. The American Popular Revolutionary Alliance (APRA), which was the hallmark of Peruvian politics for nearly four decades and served as a prototype for indigenous reform movements elsewhere in the hemisphere, came into existence as a reaction to the dictatorship of Augusto Leguía, who governed the country from 1919 to 1930. Defrauded of electoral victory in 1931 and 1936, the party was outlawed by successive military Presidents. When strongman Oscar Benavides died shortly before the 1945 elections, the Apristas were allowed to participate, and they provided the bulk of votes which elevated José Luis Bustamante to the Presidency. Subsequent conflict between Bustamante and APRA provided the opportunity for General Manuel Odría to seize power in 1948. For nearly eight years Peru prospered economically under a mild military dictatorship.

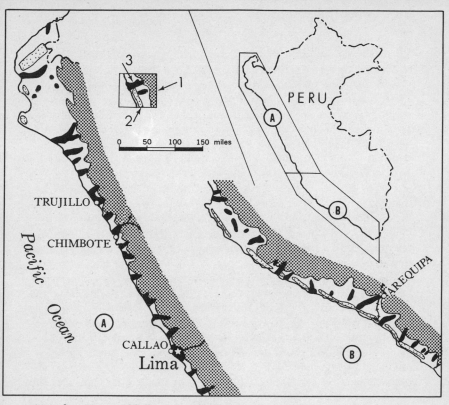

1—Andes; 2—coastal hills; 3—irrigated oasis

In the 1956 elections, APRA formed an alliance with conservative Manuel Prado and subsequently cooperated with his administration. In 1962, the party's own candidate, Víctor Raúl Haya de la Torre fell just short of the required one-third plurality, in a close race with Odría and reformist Fernando Belaúnde Terry. The APRA-hating military subsequently took power, but permitted new elections at the end of one year. This time Belaúnde, with the help of the Christian Democrats, moved past Haya and was duly inaugurated. With APRA and its old foe Odría controlling Congress, but with the apparent support of the military, Belaúnde has set out to modernize the nation and to integrate the rural population into its life. Here, too, guerrilla bands are active.

38. The Inca Empire

What is today southern Peru was five centuries ago the center of one of the world's great civilizations. At the height of its power, the Empire of the Incas embraced the area from lower Colombia to central Chile and incorporated a large variety of subject peoples. Although in cultural achievement the Incas may have surpassed the Spanish adventurers who arrived in 1531, they were no match in military technology. Moreover, Francisco Pizarro and his small band of conquistadores appeared precisely at a time when the Empire was weakened by civil strife stemming from a succession crisis. As a result, the capital of Cuzco and its rich dependencies fell to the Spaniards within less than three years. Yet a knowledge of the Inca civilization is essential to an understanding of modern-day Peru, Ecuador, and Bolivia, for more than 10 million Indians in these countries have not yet been integrated into national life and in many ways follow the heritage of their Inca ancestors.

The Inca Empire was a benevolent despotism based upon communal principles. Private property was all but unknown and the needs of the state took priority over individual desires. Society was collectivistic but sharply stratified. Free choice existed only at the very peak of the social pyramid. Products of the fields—chiefly corn, potatoes, grains, beans and peppers—were divided equally among the priests, the government, and the people, with the first two building up stores of surplus against possible famine. *Chicha*, a beer made from corn, and the narcotic coca leaf brightened the days and nights of the workers in preconquest days as at the present time, but also brought the problems of alcoholism and addiction. Incan engineers constructed roads, cities, fortifications, terraces, and irrigation works, many of which have lasted through the centuries. The domesticated llama and alpaca not only furnished meat and wool, but also served, although within strict limits, as beasts of burden. Wheeled vehicles were unknown, as was writing; messages were transmitted by means of knotted cords carried by runners over an impressive network of paved footpaths cut through the mountains. Copper and bronze utensils and weapons were abundant, but the use of iron had not been discovered.

The Spanish conquest did not greatly change the life of the highland Indian masses. The white masters who replaced the Inca nobles were often less paternalistic, but this was frequently a matter of degree. The typical Indian community, or ayllu, had generally been preserved under the Inca Empire, and it became the basis for the conquerors' holdings. In many cases, the relatively autonomous community sur-

Broken line indicates eastern border of Inca Empire

vived the colonial period and in modified form it is the basis of social
organization and economic life today in much of the Andean highlands.

39. Mineral Reserves of Peru and Bolivia

Mining is far and away the chief commercial activity in the mountain region of Peru. Even so, less than 10 per cent of the labor force is employed in mining or related activities; the vast majority of the highland population continues to live much as it did before independence or even under the Incas. Yet the mines have brought roads and railroads as well as capital to develop commercial crops and a few local industries. Peru is the second largest producer of lead and copper in Latin America (behind Mexico and Chile, respectively), and is fourth in the production of iron ore. Mineral exports earn nearly as much for Peru as cotton and sugar.

Although there have been recent major discoveries of copper in southern Peru, most of the mines are situated in the northern part of the country. Petroleum comes from the coastal area near the Ecuadorian border; copper, gold, and silver are found inland from Trujillo. With coal available in adequate supplies, the ores are processed and smelted before being sent by rail to the ports. Iron is abundant near Chimbote, a rapidly growing city of 150,000 inhabitants, and some of it is made into steel for domestic use. The richest mines have traditionally been associated with Cerro de Pasco, where as far back as 1630 silver was packed on mules for the trip to Lima. In the nineteenth century, a railroad was built over a pass at nearly 16,000 feet to reach the mines, which by then were producing copper, lead, zinc, gold, and mercury in addition to silver. Much of these mineral riches are in the hands of U.S. companies, whose total investments are near $500 million.

Bolivia is even more dependent upon mineral resources than is its neighbor. Tin, produced chiefly in nationalized mines, accounts for three-fourths of government revenues and an even higher proportion of exports. Lead, zinc, copper, and silver are also found in commercial quantities. Unfortunately, the condition of the mines (Bolivia's tin mines are located at such extreme altitudes that only Indians from the Altiplano can work them, and health and safety practices leave much to be desired), an excessively large and politically potent labor force, and the high cost of long-distance rail shipment to Chilean ports combine to keep Bolivian tin only marginally competitive—indeed, the state mining corporation operates with a chronic deficit. In view of this, many Bolivians feel that the ore should be smelted within the country rather than sent to Great Britain. Friction between militant unions and foreign technicians brought in to improve efficiency and modernize the mines has also been a serious problem in recent years. Proposals to cut the labor force or to eliminate subsidized commissaries have repeatedly

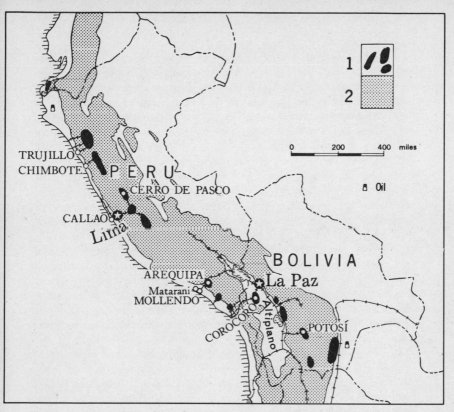

1—major mining areas; 2—Andes

brought the leftist-led miners to the point of rebellion. Civilian governments have been reluctant to clash with the workers' militia, but the present military regime has taken a tougher stand.

Petroleum resources in the eastern lowlands are being exploited by both the Bolivian Government and U.S. and Brazilian firms. Production is still quite low, and it is uncertain whether petroleum will become a major export. Silver mines at Potosí, in colonial days the richest in the world, have been all but exhausted, although with more than 60,000 inhabitants the city is still the center of varied mining activities. But its rich mineral resources have not been sufficient to lift Bolivia out of its unenviable spot as the third poorest Latin American republic in terms of per capita gross national products, ahead only of Haiti and Paraguay and far behind neighboring Chile, Brazil, Argentina, and Peru.

40.   The Other Side of the Mountains

At least half of Peru and three-fifths of Bolivia lie east of the Andes and face the interior of South America. Although relatively well endowed in terms of soil and climate and traversed by adequate rivers, this potentially productive area is all but uninhabited. Although the highlands population is reluctant to colonize the region because of the differences in altitude and temperature, the major barrier to development is lack of transportation. Iquitos, the sixth largest city of Peru, with a population of over 60,000, is located in this area, but has always been more accessible from the Atlantic, 2,300 miles away by steamer up the Amazon, than from other Peruvian centers. Air transportation, however, is rapidly changing this, and the Belaúnde government has embarked on an ambitious program of road building to supplement the highway which now reaches Pucallpa, crossing the Andes at nearly 16,000 feet. Just as the rubber boom at the end of the nineteenth century led to an increase in the population of this part of Peru, the search for oil may provide an economic impetus for settlement; if not, demographic pressures eventually will. The present population of trans-Andean Peru includes some 500,000 Indians. The large department of Loreto, which includes the city of Iquitos, has only one inhabitant per square kilometer.

In Bolivia, the semitropical lowland *Yungas,* with their fertile soils, lie only 200 miles northeast of La Paz, yet transportation of their foodstuffs to the capital is hindered by mountains that rise as high as 20,000 feet. Moreover, preference is given to the cultivation of coca, whose leaves the Indians chew as a relatively mild form of narcotic. Farther north, open plains, frequently flooded, and the dense forests of Beni and Pando remain essentially untouched, and the few transportation routes that do exist lead toward Brazil and not into the center of the country; some road building is, however, being carried out by the Bolivian army. The grasslands around Santa Cruz are somewhat better linked by roads to the Altiplano, but here a main avenue of communication is by rail to the Brazilian city of Corumbá on the Paraguay River. In recent years, the discovery and exploitation of petroleum, albeit on a small scale, has served as a catalyst in the development of this region. Open ranching prevails in the Chaco. Although Bolivia has even greater need than Peru to incorporate its eastern territory into the national economy, it almost totally lacks the necessary financial resources. Moreover, it has been a heavy borrower for other pressing needs. Nonetheless, settlement is slowly taking place. A large number of Oki-

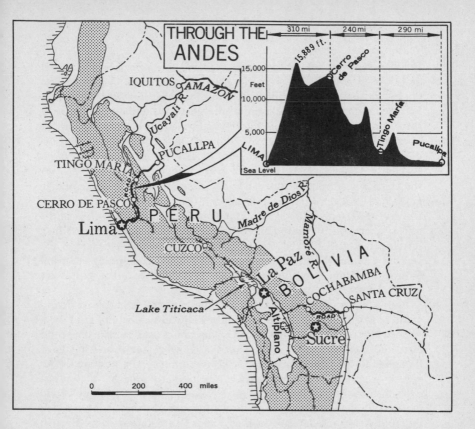

nawan immigrants, coming by way of Brazil, now cultivate sugar cane and rice, and perhaps 200,000 highland *campesinos* have also moved into the lowland areas.

41. Bolivia

Bolivian experience has clearly demonstrated that a social revolution in and of itself is not the answer to a country's problems. Despite a thorough-going national revolution initiated in 1952, Bolivia continues to be faced with a depressing array of problems. Straddling the Andes at their widest point, Bolivia is the only fully landlocked country in the Western Hemisphere. (Paraguay, although it has no seacoast, has access to the sea through the Paraguay River.) Almost three-quarters of its nearly 4.3 million inhabitants live at altitudes of over 10,000 feet; the chief concentrations are near Lake Titicaca on the Altiplano, which is really a series of high altitude basins. The capital of La Paz, which has grown to some 400,000 inhabitants, is situated at 12,000 feet in the midst of an essentially Indian population. Cochabamba, located in a fertile valley at 8,400 feet, boasts a population of 100,000 and is the center of an increasingly mestizo cultural region. The mining center of Oruro and Santa Cruz on the eastern lowlands are other significant urban centers, both nearing the 100,000 mark.

Bolivia has traditionally been one of the least stable and least democratic of the Latin American republics. Political power was held by a small white upper class which owned the mines and most of the good land and controlled the army. The disastrous defeat at the hands of Paraguay in the Chaco War (1932–35) undermined the position of the elite and gave rise to demands for revolutionary change. Through a coup in December, 1943, a group of young officers came to power in partnership with the Nationalist Revolutionary Movement (MNR), led by middle-class intellectuals such as Víctor Paz Estenssoro and Hernán Siles Zuazo. Ousted by force in 1946, the MNR won the 1951 elections; although denied the fruits of their electoral victory, the MNR came to power the following year through a successful revolution. The army was virtually destroyed, the oligarchy stripped of its privileges, and major efforts were made to incorporate the miners and peasants into the life of the nation. The tin mines were nationalized and a substantial agrarian reform implemented.

In 1956, Siles was elected to succeed Paz as President. Attempting, with large-scale U.S. assistance, to halt inflation and develop the Bolivian economy, Siles came into conflict with Juan Lechín, leader of the radical wing of the MNR. After 1958, elections became increasingly manipulated. At the same time, the armed forces were strengthened as violence in the countryside and among the miners rose. Paz's electoral victory in 1960 caused defections by MNR conservatives. Dissension within the government party increased during Paz's second administration; when he decided to seek re-election in 1964, both

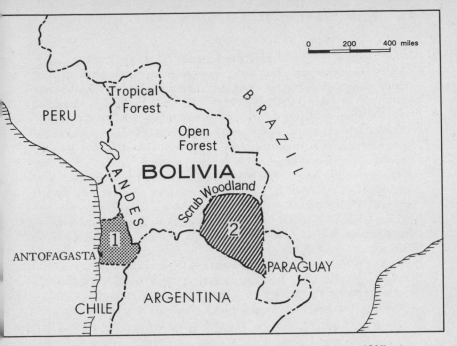

1—territory lost to Chile in 1884; *2*—territory lost to Paraguay in 1935

Lechín and Siles went into opposition and boycotted the elections. On November 4, 1964, Paz was overthrown by his new Vice President, General René Barrientos, who has since headed a provisional government.

Bolivia's economic problems remain essentially as grave as they were a decade ago. Relatively little progress has been made in diversification, and tin is produced at a cost above world market prices. The mines are sorely in need of modernization, but the government lacks the requisite capital. Infrastructure investments have not yet had readily apparent beneficial effects, and the tropical forests of the northeast, eastern lowlands, and southeastern woodlands have not been put to productive use. A continued heavy inflow of foreign assistance (over $400 million from the United States alone since 1952) has prevented marked economic deterioration, and similar transfusions will be needed for many years to come.

42. Chile: History and Politics

In any discussion of Latin America, Chileans like to point out that their country is an exception, and there is more than a little truth to their refrain. Geographically this elongated land stretches over 2,500 miles from north to south (the equivalent of California to Alaska), averaging only 100 miles in width; the bulk of its 8.5 million inhabitants are concentrated in the central section. Although great numbers are engaged in agriculture, it is the minerals of the barren deserts that provide essential foreign-exchange earnings—copper alone accounts for two-thirds of Chile's exports. Thirty-five per cent white and the remainder mestizo, Chileans ethnically have much more in common with Argentina and Uruguay than with the other Andean republics. Like the former, Chile is relatively urbanized, with more than half its population clustered around Santiago, now a city of more than 2 million inhabitants.

Chile has the best record of constitutional government and free elections of any major Latin American nation. Indeed, under the leadership of Diego Portales a pattern of national politics based upon stability without dictatorship was established as early as the 1830's. By mid-century, new parties with meaningful programs were enriching the traditional Liberal-Conservative division. Coastal commercial groups and northern mining interests gained in political influence. Gradually a new middle class and urban working groups became factors of some weight. In contrast to other Latin American countries, Congress steadily gained strength in relation to the executive, and it became dominant following a brief civil war in 1891. During the next three decades the governing elite provided orderly national progress and a tradition of constitutionality.

The contemporary era of political change dates from 1920, when Arturo Alessandri was elected President. Coming to power when the collapse of the nitrate market had brought widespread unemployment, Alessandri pushed through basic reform programs and a new constitution abolishing parliamentary government. Following a seven-year period of military dictatorship and popular unrest, Alessandri returned to power in 1932, bringing order and economic recovery during the next four years. Subsequently, Chile had a series of "Popular Front" coalition governments led by the essentially middle-class Radical Party. Popular disenchantment led to the election of ex-dictator Carlos Ibáñez in 1952. Six years later, victory went to Jorge Alessandri, an independent backed by rightist parties, in an extremely close contest. The September, 1964, election was a race between the two candidates who had challenged Alessandri in 1958: Christian Democrat Eduardo Frei and

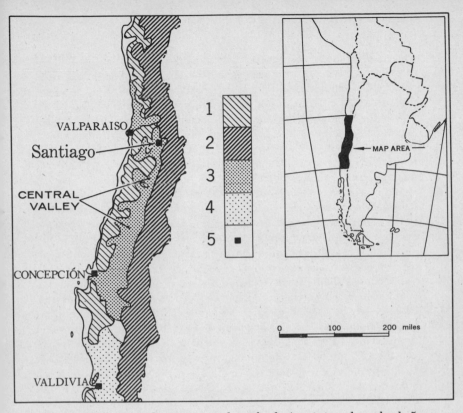

1—coastal hills; *2*—Andes; *3*—irrigated cropland; *4*—unirrigated cropland; *5*—industrial city

pro-Castro Marxist Salvador Allende, backed by the Communist-Socialist alliance. Chilean Conservatives this time supported the former instead of running their own candidate. Frei's resounding victory by a better than three-to-two margin gave new confidence to democratic reform forces throughout Latin America, and the Christian Democratic triumph in the March, 1965, congressional elections focused hemispheric attention upon the progress of the new administration, dedicated to bringing about a nonviolent social revolution. This does not promise to be an easy task, but the Frei administration appears to be attacking the country's serious economic problems in a vigorous and intelligent manner.

43. Regions of Chile

The most intensively developed part of Chile is the "Central Valley," in reality a series of fertile valleys and basins lying between the main cordillera of the Andes and the lower coastal ranges. With much of the best land held in large estates and used for grazing and vineyards, demands for agrarian reform have been steadily growing. The necessary legislation is now on the books, and the requisite institutions have been established. With peasants and rural workers organizing to defend their interests and many landlords intransigent, tension has mounted in the countryside. Population pressures are also increasing, resulting in large-scale migration to the cities; nearly 65 per cent of all Chileans are now urban dwellers. While no city rivals the capital, Valparaiso has grown to nearly 300,000 and Concepción to nearly 200,000. Six other cities have populations around 100,000. Industrialization has also gone forward, particularly in the consumer-goods field, and Concepción boasts one of the continent's major steel plants.

Despite considerable diversification in recent decades, economic development remains seriously unbalanced. A net importer of foodstuffs, Chile is heavily dependent upon mineral exports. The country's prosperity stemmed largely from acquisition of rich nitrate resources through conquest from Peru and Bolivia in the War of the Pacific (1879–83), and the collapse of the international nitrate markets in the 1920's set back economic growth and ushered in a period of political turmoil. Subsequently copper has moved into the position of dominance in the export field. With an estimated 30 per cent of world copper reserves, Chile is responsible for some 15 per cent of actual production. Sales of nitrates and iron bring in only one-fourth as much foreign exchange as copper. The copper mines are chiefly U.S.–owned, and there is a widespread demand for increased national control and benefits. The present administration has negotiated agreements with the major copper companies providing for substantial new investment and government participation in ownership and management.

Although the Central Valley is the country's heartland, the other regions have an important economic role to play. The arid northern provinces provide two-thirds of the copper production in addition to all of the nitrates and iron ore. Southern Chile, which contains one-third of all arable land, furnishes over half of all agricultural output, has significant manufacturing, and is the source of the country's coal. The region near Punta Arenas, the world's southernmost city, produces enough crude oil to meet two-thirds of Chile's growing need for petroleum.

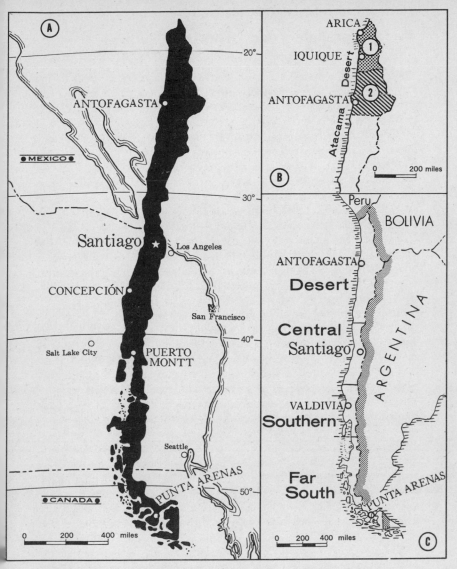

A. Chile superimposed on western North America at the same latitudes
B. *Desert Chile:* 1—territory gained from Peru; 2—territory gained from Bolivia
C. Regions of Chile

44.   Geographical and Historical Features

Common geographical and historical factors have contributed to the
similarity of the three Atlantic-oriented countries of Spanish South
America. The La Plata region was developed rather late in the colonial
period, due chiefly to its lack of mineral wealth. Despite the inviting
estuary of the great stream formed by the confluence of the Paraguay,
Paraná, and Uruguay rivers, the area was explored and governed from
the Pacific coast. Asunción in Paraguay was founded in 1537 by an
expedition working its way down from Peru and Bolivia, and Buenos
Aires was established more than forty years later by a group from
Asunción. Indeed, the earliest permanent settlement in what is today
Argentina was made in 1553 at Santiago del Estero by Spaniards who
had crossed the mountains from Chile. Only the northern third of the
country was colonized before independence, and this by emigrants
from the more developed Andean settlements. Although Argentina
now boasts a population in excess of 22 million, nearly three times
that of Chile, the latter was the more populous until the 1870's.

After the original arc of frontier settlements was finished, nearly two
centuries passed before the region became Europe-oriented. In 1777,
Buenos Aires finally became a viceregal capital; within a few decades
it was the center of an independent country. Between 1829 and 1852,
dictator Juan Manuel de Rosas brought the city and the provinces together into the beginnings of a real nation. After his fall, a series of
liberal Presidents carried on the work of integration. By 1880, all the
Pampa area was occupied, and a series of military campaigns subsequently opened the way for the frontier to move southward as far as
Patagonia. European immigration, which helped the Argentine population double between 1850 and 1880, also swallowed up the relatively
small mestizo elements. In the two decades between 1890 and 1910,
it was the basis for another 100 per cent population increase. As the
land began to fill up, Spanish and Italian immigrants settled in the burgeoning city of Buenos Aires with its opportunities for industrial employment.

Uruguay was colonized from Brazil during the latter part of the
seventeenth century. To limit Portuguese expansion southward, the
Spaniards established Montevideo as a military outpost in 1726. This
area, commonly known as the *Banda Oriental*, remained a focus of
Luso-Iberian rivalry until after the wars of independence, and in 1828
it became an independent buffer state between the Argentine Republic

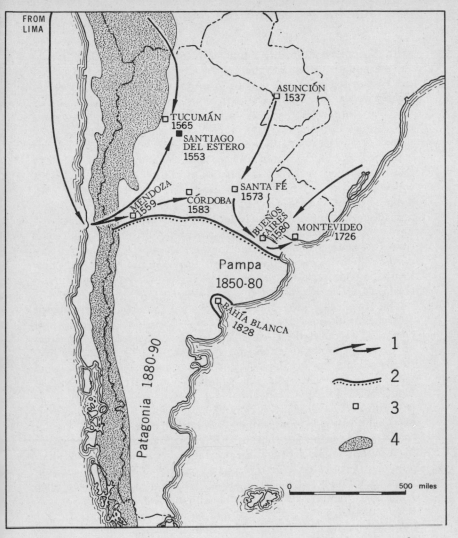

FROM
LIMA

ASUNCIÓN
1537

TUCUMÁN
1565
SANTIAGO
DEL ESTERO
1553

MENDOZA
1559
CÓRDOBA
1583

SANTA FÉ
1573

BUENOS
AIRES
1580

MONTEVIDEO
1726

Pampa
1850-80

BAHÍA BLANCA
1828

Patagonia 1880-90

1

2

3

4

0   500 miles

1—main Spanish and Portuguese immigration routes; 2—approximate southern limit of settlement, to 1850; 3—early Spanish settlement and date of
establishment; 4—Andes

and the Brazilian Empire. Its population grew chiefly through immigration from Spain and Italy.

45. Buenos Aires and the Pampa

With a population of nearly 7 million in its metropolitan area, Buenos Aires is one of the world's great cities. The political capital of one of the Western Hemisphere's major nations, it is also the most important combination port and industrial city in all Latin America. Often called the "Paris of South America," it is the continent's cultural capital and enjoys a temperate climate. In conjunction with its hinterland, the fabled Argentine Pampa, it comprises some 15 million persons and a combined agricultural-manufacturing output matched only by Brazil's São Paulo region (*see Map 53*). Buenos Aires itself contains the largest concentration of organized labor in Latin America. Its packing plants, grain elevators, warehouses, and railroad yards handle the area's vast agricultural production; its factories are oriented toward the large domestic market. The area has limited mineral resources; fuel must come from Patagonia, and most of the iron ore for its steel industry is imported along with many other industrial raw materials. With tariff protection, a wide variety of consumer goods, as well as machinery and chemicals, are locally produced.

The Pampa is a level grasslands covering the area within roughly 400 miles of Buenos Aires. With its deep and fertile soils and favorable climate it resembles the Great Plains of the United States. Vast areas of the Pampa are used for wheat, corn, and pasture crops, while livestock predominates in other sections. The evolution of the area is not unlike that of much of the U.S. Middle West. Extensive ranching of tough, half-wild cattle predominated in the nineteenth century while population was still relatively light. Transportation problems and market conditions made hides, rather than beef, the chief export. The introduction of refrigerator ships in 1877 changed all this, and large-scale meat exports to Great Britain were instituted. Packing plants proliferated and range cattle were replaced by pure-bred Herefords and animals carefully chosen for their meat. Barbed wire divided the open ranges and farming came to coexist with grazing. Large numbers of immigrants began to raise wheat and corn. While Argentina did not have an exact equivalent of the U.S. Homestead Act to speed the process, the number of independent farms did grow, and many of the large *estancias* have been divided by sale and inheritance. Thus both family farms and latifundia worked by tenants are common in the Pampa. The large landowner or *estanciero* class no longer dominates the economic and political life, or even the social order. Much of this development is tied up with the story of political change (*see Map 47*).

In addition to the Buenos Aires metropolis, a number of other major cities lie within the Pampa. Rosario, which with 700,000 inhabitants is

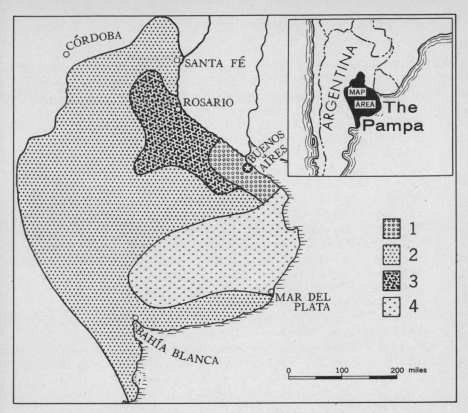

1—truck gardening (fruits and vegetables); *2*—alfalfa and wheat; *3*—corn; *4*—pasture

Argentina's second city, is the center of the nation's belt, in the midst of land so productive that per acre yields of wheat and flax are also the country's highest. As a river port and rail center, it is one of the country's major transportation hubs. Santa Fé, a city of over 200,000, on the upper rim of the Pampa, serves as gateway to the Argentine Northeast. La Plata, with some 350,000 inhabitants, serves the capital as an auxiliary port, while Bahia Blanca is the commercial and transportation center for the lower Pampa, nearly 400 miles from Buenos Aires.

46. Interior Argentina

Although Buenos Aires and the Pampa are the core of the Argentine nation, the several regions of the interior each have a significant contribution to make. The eastern slope of the Andes, with its scattered settlements dating from the sixteenth century, is still oriented to some extent toward Chile. While the mineral wealth of the Argentine ranges does not match that of the Pacific side, there is significant production of lead, zinc, and copper along with lesser metals such as asbestos and beryllium needed by the United States. Petroleum fields are also found along the piedmont. Just to the east of the Andes lies Tucumán, now a city of over 300,000 inhabitants, and Mendoza, about half this size. The former is the heart of the sugar-producing area, which supplies the country's large demands—as much as 800,000 tons a year. The latter, much closer to Santiago than to Buenos Aires, is the center of the country's wine industry. Here again the internal market provided by the populous east is sufficient to absorb production. Range cattle graze in the semi-arid grasslands between the oases.

The Argentine Northeast, comprising chiefly forests and grasslands, was long linked with Paraguay and Uruguay, rather than with the Andean countries. The sections known as Mesopotamia, lying between the Paraná and Uruguay rivers, and the Argentine Chaco are agricultural areas. The former is the country's source of maté, drunk in preference to tea; the latter provides quebracho wood, from which tannin is extracted, and most of the country's cotton—in Latin America, only Brazil and Mexico now oustrip Argentina in cotton production. Córdoba, a strong challenger of Rosario for the honor of being the country's second city, contains an estimated 650,000 persons. Situated on the edge of the wheat belt, it is a major transportation hub and center of an extensive ranching area.

The largest but least developed region is Patagonia, an area of chilly, wind-swept plateaus generally too cold and dry for successful farming. Despite efforts at settlement by immigrants from Great Britain during the closing decades of the nineteenth century, it is still very sparsely inhabited. Except along a few rivers flowing from the Andes, where irrigation makes fruit growing possible, little of this land is in crops; the area's chief economic activity is sheepherding. However, the nation's main producing oil fields are found in Patagonia, and the lake district in the Andean foothills is being developed as a vacation land.

Argentina claims a major portion of Antarctica and some border areas in dispute with Chile. The Falkland Islands, known to the Argentines as the Malvinas, have been a major bone of contention with the

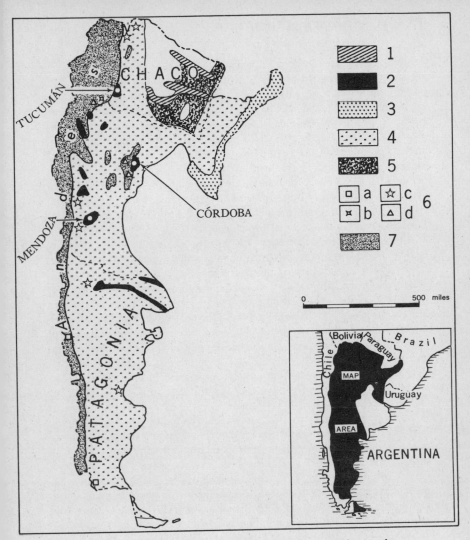

1—cotton; 2—irrigated agriculture (sugar cane, fruits, etc.); 3—other crop agriculture; 4—livestock ranching; 5—quebracho; 6—*mineral deposits:* a—coal; b—copper; c—petroleum; d—tungsten; 7—mountain areas

British for a century. On Argentine maps they are designated as "occupied territory."

47. Argentine Political Life

Argentina presents the perplexing case of a country which, after making substantial progress toward a wide-based political democracy, has proved unable to cope with further problems of political change. Following the final defeat of dictator Rosas, in 1852, Argentina experienced a prolonged period of civilian government by enlightened members of the elite. By the 1890's, however, industrialization, urbanization, immigration, and education brought into being new political movements opposed to the continued dominance of the large landowners. Through electoral fraud, the Conservatives held on to control of the government until one from their own ranks, Roque Sáenz Peña, engineered electoral reforms which enabled the essentially middle-class Radical Civic Union to come to power in 1916.

Although the administration of Radical leader Hipólito Irigoyen could claim substantial accomplishments, subsequent divisions within the party prevented it from uniting the middle class and urban working masses behind a program of democracy, nationalism, and social welfare. As a result of the inability of President Irigoyen to deal with the impact of the world depression of 1930, radicalism was largely discredited. Thus, those elements in the military which were disdainful of constitutional representative democracy were able to seize power, and the country entered a period of retrogression. General José Uriburu, although unable to impose a fascist regime based on the Italian model he so admired, did pave the way for the "infamous decade" of Conservative emasculation of democracy, which led to a subsequent takeover by the neofascist elements within the military.

By 1943, few Argentines were prepared to oppose a sweeping change in the political order, and ostensibly democratic institutions were quite thoroughly discredited. Within two years of the army's seizing power, Colonel Juan Domingo Perón emerged as the regime's dominant figure and a popular leader such as the country had never known. Perón cast himself as the champion of the urban workers, whose ranks had multiplied during the rapid industrialization of the 1930's and who were deeply resentful of a political system responsive to the interests of the large agricultural proprietors. Elected to the Presidency in 1946, he subsequently built up a mass Peronista party and labor movement which insured his re-election in 1951. After the death of his wife and political right arm, the demagogic Evita Perón, in July, 1952, the Argentine dictator found it increasingly difficult to satisfy the desires of both labor and the military. Moreover, the artificial prosperity of the immediate postwar period had come to an end. Unrealistic overemphasis of industrialization had further unbalanced the economy, and

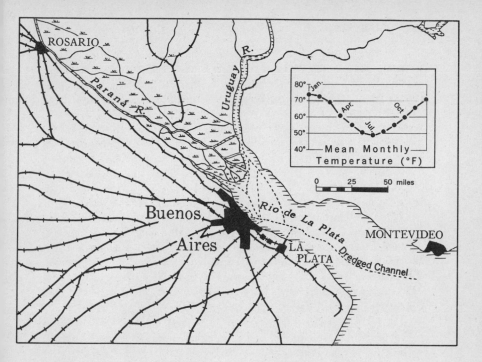

hundreds of thousands of recent arrivals from the countryside had been added to the ranks of urban workers who expected ever greater economic benefits. His popularity partially eroded, Perón was overthrown by a military revolt in September, 1955.

Arturo Frondizi, an "Intransigent" Radical elected President in February, 1958, owed his victory in large part to Peronist votes. Reversing many of his nationalistic campaign stances, Frondizi followed orthodox economic policies in trying to cope with the chaos he had inherited and walked a tightrope between labor and the military. Following congressional elections in which the Peronistas were permitted to participate and in which they scored impressive gains, Frondizi was ousted by the armed forces in March, 1962. In the general elections of July, 1963, Dr. Arturo Illia of the Popular Radical Civic Union was elected President with only 25 per cent of the popular vote. Peronist blank votes, however, were under 20 per cent of the total for the first time since the dictator's fall. During his initial years in office as a minority President, Illia faced essentially the same problems as had Frondizi. Reintegration of the Peronistas remained a major barrier to a resumption of progress and development. Indeed, the supporters of Perón made a strong showing in the March, 1965, congressional elections.

48. Uruguay

Uruguay has long enjoyed a reputation as one of Latin America's most democratic and progressive countries. Moreover, its fewer than 3 million citizens, chiefly of European descent, enjoy a relatively high standard of living. Montevideo, with a population of nearly 1.3 million, is one of the continent's more prosperous cities and dominates national life. (No other urban center contains as many as 70,000 persons.) Yet the economy is highly agrarian, with wool, hides, and meat accounting for about 90 per cent of export trade. Some 25 million sheep and 10 million cattle populate the grazing lands of this small country and give it the highest relation of livestock to land area in Latin America.

With little sense of nationhood at the time of independence (which was engineered largely by the British), Uruguay was in many respects a pawn in the Brazilian-Argentine power struggle until after 1870. Its political life was marked by instability until after the turn of the century, although progress toward orderly representative government was made through the two permanent political parties, the Colorados and the Blancos. José Batlle y Ordóñez, first elected President in 1903, dominated the political scene until his death in 1929 and engineered the establishment of a thoroughly Social-Democratic regime with heavy emphasis on social welfare. By encouraging state intervention in the economy, he also spurred the development of a large middle class, the majority of whom are government employees. Following a brief dictatorial interlude in the 1930's, democratic government has functioned reasonably well except in the field of economic productivity and growth. The country's unique plural executive—a nine-man National Council of Government in which the majority party is granted six seats and the minority party three—and factionalization within the parties have led to immobilism. Generally speaking, the Blancos, who have won the last two elections, are more conservative and less urban-oriented than the Colorados. Their 1958 victory was something of an upset and their margin in 1962 paper thin; with continued economic stagnation, a Colorado win in the next election is a real possibility.

The accomplishments of the Uruguayan welfare state are impressive. The country's wealth has been distributed so that a very sizable proportion of the population enjoys economic security and human dignity. Freedom from want is more universal than in any other Latin American country. Yet the system is now facing serious difficulties. Living standards and social benefits have outstripped productivity and have continued at artificially high levels. Although the effects of economic stagnation have not yet been felt in full force, due to the cushioning impact of social security and other government programs, a

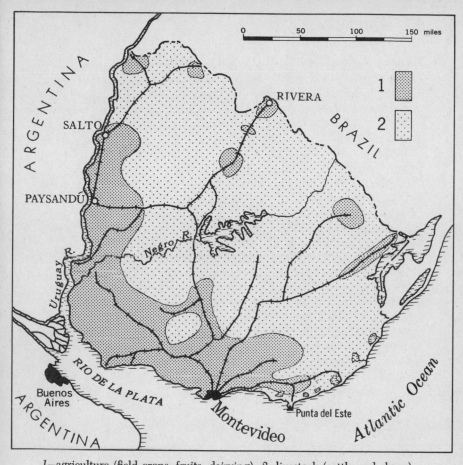

1—agriculture (field crops, fruits, dairying); 2—livestock (cattle and sheep)

reckoning must eventually come. Chronic trade deficits, continued low prices and deterioration of the market for Uruguay exports, and substantial inflation cannot be wished away. Many of the present university generation consider the programs of the established parties sterile and are turning toward Communism. Even the Uruguayan armed forces, considered by many observers the most nonpolitical in South America, appear increasingly restive. Support is growing for abolition of the plural executive and establishment of a strong Presidency.

49. Paraguay

Paraguay has long been one of the least fortunate countries of Latin America. Its nearly 2 million inhabitants exist on a per capita income even lower than that of their Bolivian neighbors. Asunción, with more than 300,000 inhabitants, is perhaps the most provincial of the continent's capitals. Three-quarters of all Paraguayans live within 100 miles of Asunción, and the country's second city has not yet reached the 50,000 mark. The two-thirds of Paraguay's territory lying west of the Paraguay River has so far proved of little value—certainly not enough to justify the lives lost in wresting this dry plain (the Chaco) from Bolivia. Although lacking a seacoast, Paraguay is not landlocked in the same sense as Bolivia; each year hundreds of ships come up the Paraguay River from Buenos Aires, some 1,000 miles downstream. Not surprisingly, Argentina is the chief trading partner, followed by the United States. Although essentially an agricultural economy and with abundant unused arable land, Paraguay regularly imports some foodstuffs. Its principal exports are meat and forest products at an annual rate of less than $25 per person, one of the lowest in the hemisphere.

The Paraguayans are overwhelmingly mestizo. During the sixteenth century, the Spaniards conquered the peaceful Guaraní Indians, and Guaraní blood still is predominant in the resulting racial mixture; the Guaraní language is also in common usage throughout the country. Class distinctions are of markedly less importance than in most other Latin American countries.

Paraguay has spent more of its life as a nation under dictators than has any other South American country, and is still the most retarded politically. For three full decades after independence, José Gaspar Rodríguez de Francia, self-styled "Supreme One," closed Paraguay to the outside world. His successor, Carlos Antonio López, governed for twenty-one years. The latter's son, Francisco Solana López, brought disaster to the country by provoking war with Brazil, Argentina, and Uruguay; when he was finally slain in battle in 1870, only 28,000 Paraguayan men remained alive out of more than a quarter-million.

From three heads of government in sixty years, Paraguay went to the other extreme—forty Presidents in the next eighty years. Although nominally the victor in the Chaco war, which ended in 1935, the country's male population was again decimated. In 1940, General Higinio Morénigo entrenched himself in power, surviving a six-month civil war in 1947. After three interim Presidents in one year, Federico Chávez was elected in 1950. Four years later the present epoch began as Army Chief of Staff Alfredo Stroessner took over the Presidency, following a coup and an "uncontested" election. Re-elected in 1958

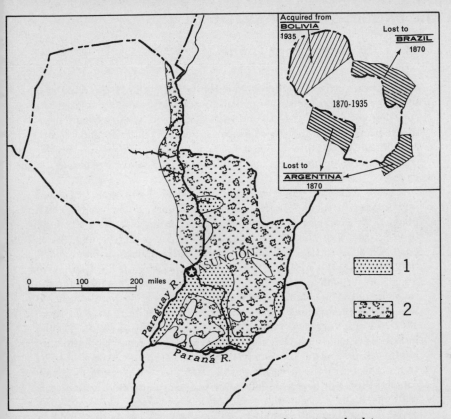

1—major cropland; 2—forest and grazing; most of remaining land is swamp and shrub of little or no economic value

and again in 1963, the Paraguayan strongman appears disposed to hold power as long as possible. Although a token opposition faction was given one-third of the seats in Congress in the last election, most of the real opponents of the regime have been forced into exile. Indeed, an estimated 300,000 Paraguayans now live across the river in Argentina. The nature of the Stroessner government can be seen from the fact that all army officers are members of the official party.

THE UNITED STATES OF BRAZIL

50.   An Adolescent Giant

The vast expanse of Brazil covers nearly half of all South America, and the more than 80 million Brazilians numerically equal the Spanish-speaking population of the continent. Combined with substantial industrialization, rich and varied resources, and a relatively good record of political stability and adherence to constitutional processes, this has convinced Brazilians that their country should be recognized as an emerging world power.

Having secured its independence without civil war or a protracted revolutionary struggle, Brazil was spared most of the strife which plagued its Hispanic American neighbors throughout the nineteenth century (see Map 10). Its nearly seven decades of independent existence as a constitutional monarchy established a pattern of internal stability that continued under the "Old Republic" (1889–1930). Political and economic crises in the late 1920's paved the way for the revolution of 1930, which brought Getúlio Vargas to power and ushered in a period of sustained social, economic, and political change. From 1930 to 1945, Vargas governed Brazil as a benevolent dictator, pushing industrialization, improving the position of urban labor, and strengthening the powers of the federal government at the expense of the states. Ousted by the armed forces in 1945, he won election as constitutional President five years later, but was unable to cope successfully with the manifold economic and political problems. On August 24, 1954, Vargas committed suicide rather than comply with a military ultimatum to resign.

The 1955 Presidential elections resulted in the victory of Vargas' political heirs, the moderate Juscelino Kubitschek and his leftist running mate, João Goulart. Kubitschek embarked on an ambitious program of economic development designed to bring Brazil "fifty years' progress in five" and a more vigorous foreign policy. As vast quantities of new currency were issued to pay for these programs, Brazil's chronic inflation began to spiral. Promising to continue Brazil's rapid economic growth while at the same time setting the country's financial and administrative house in order, Jânio Quadros gained a landslide victory in the 1960 Presidential balloting.

Quadros dashed the hopes of the millions who saw him as the nation's political messiah when he abruptly resigned after only seven months in office. The resulting crisis was compromised in a typically Brazilian manner by permitting Goulart to assume the Presidency after the adoption of a modified parliamentary system of government had

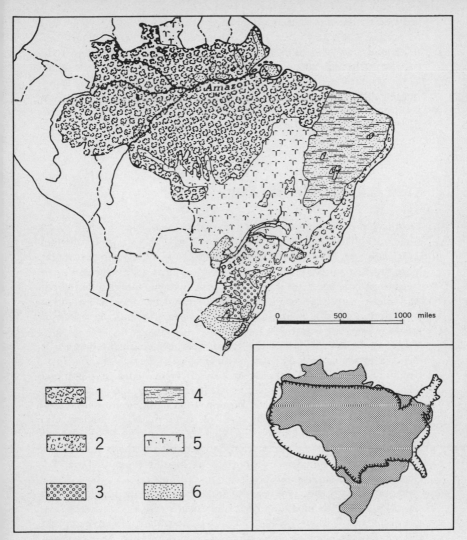

1—tropical rain forest; 2—tropical deciduous forest; 3—temperate mixed forest; 4—scrub woodland; 5—grassland with trees; 6—prairie
Inset map shows the conterminous United States superimposed on Brazil

reduced the powers of that office. Goulart's actions during the closing months of 1963 and early 1964 convinced most of the military and influential state governors that he was taking the country down the road to a leftist dictatorship. Their successful revolt in April, 1964, led to the establishment of a government headed by retired Marshal Humberto Castelo Branco, who is to hold power until the elections now scheduled for November, 1966.

51.   A Racial Melting Pot

Brazilians proudly assert that their nation is the world's leading racial democracy. This claim is essentially justified, although social distinctions based on color do exist, particularly in the cities of the South. Most Brazilians believe that intermixture produces a stronger and more creative people; for them miscegenation is not something to be feared. And unlike many of its neighbors, Brazil has not restricted immigration to preferred European stock; there has been considerable influx of Japanese since the war, for example.

During the colonial period the Portuguese settlers (themselves a rich blend of European and Moorish elements) mixed freely with the Tupi-Guaraní Indians and Negro slaves brought from Africa as plantation labor. Following independence, particularly during the period from 1850 to 1930, a heavy stream of European immigration, totaling nearly 5 million, fed the rapid development of southern Brazil. Italians and Portuguese were predominant, but Spain, Germany, and Poland were also well represented. Today the descendants of these immigrants make up a very significant proportion of Brazil's expanding middle-class and professional sectors.

Despite the great diversity in the ethnic origins of its population and quite rigid class distinctions, Brazil has developed a considerable degree of national solidarity based upon homogeneity of language and religion. Its development into a modern, economically diversified nation with broad popular participation in political life has been held back by a high degree of illiteracy, serious health problems, regionalism, and the dominance of special interests. The fundamental changes which since 1930 have become so noticeable in the cities have not yet penetrated into the rural areas. Moreover, the rapid industrialization of southern Brazil has accentuated the differences between these relatively rich and advanced states and the rest of the country. Then, too, recent years have witnessed a revolution in the aspirations of the Bra-

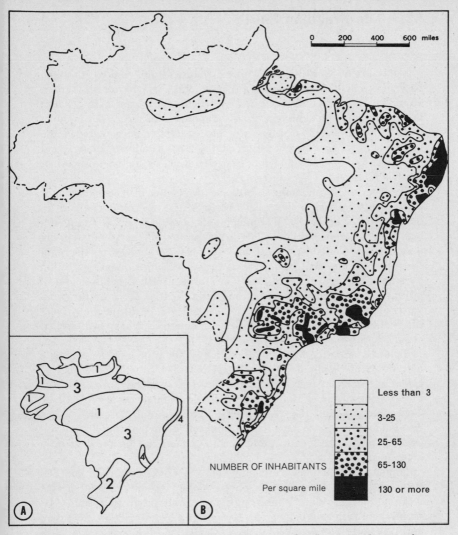

A. Racial composition of Brazil (highly generalized): 1—predominantly Indian; 2—predominantly European; 3—mixed European and Indian; 4—mixed, with a high proportion of Negroes
B. Population density

zilian people. Although many enjoy material and social advantages previously unknown, there is a widening gap between what the people have and what they feel entitled to.

109

52. The Brazilian South

Rio Grande do Sul, Santa Catarina, and Paraná—the southernmost states of Brazil—constitute an important agricultural region. Although basically rural, the area supports a population which will soon reach 15 million. Heavily influenced by German, Italian, Spanish, and Polish immigrants, and benefiting from a temperate climate, the people of the South are generally progressive and energetic. Particularly in Rio Grande do Sul excessively large estates are virtually unknown, and rural society is based upon family-sized farms, as in the Midwest of the United States.

The heart of Rio Grande do Sul, and the center of its population of more than 6 million, is its capital, Pôrto Alegre, a commercial and industrial city of nearly 750,000 inhabitants, around which is arranged a rich ethnic-economic mosaic. The lower portion of the state is largely pastoral, producing hides, wool, and salt beef. West of Pôrto Alegre, in the valley of the Rio Jacuí, rice is grown in large quantities by an essentially Portuguese population. The German settlements to the north produce corn, potatoes, tobacco, and hogs. To the north lie the vineyards of the Italians, established in the late nineteenth century. Near the northern border of the state lies the country's wheat belt, settled chiefly during the past twenty-five years.

Santa Catarina (population 2.5 million) is the source of the country's only significant coal-mining area. Coal from near Tubarão provides fuel essential to Pôrto Alegre's industrial development and partially meets the growing needs of Brazil's steel industry. Colonized after 1850 by German immigrants, the state furnishes pork and dairy products to the São Paulo and Rio de Janeiro metropolises. Light industry has developed in recent decades to provide employment for the growing farm labor surplus.

Paraná, which in many respects resembles its northern neighbor, São Paulo, is developing from a sparsely populated agricultural frontier area into one of the country's more prosperous and progressive states. Its rapidly growing population has already reached 6 million. Intensive and systematic colonization began only after 1876; in subsequent decades, heavy Polish, Russian, and German immigration (the latter from Santa Catarina, rather than from Europe) soon relegated the original Portuguese settlers to a minority position. In recent years, the northern portion of the state has been developed as the coffee-growing zone has spread southward from São Paulo. Here, around the modern and rapidly growing city of Londrina, has come into being what is perhaps the largest and most prosperous region of small, independent farmers in all Latin America. This portion of the state is still largely oriented toward

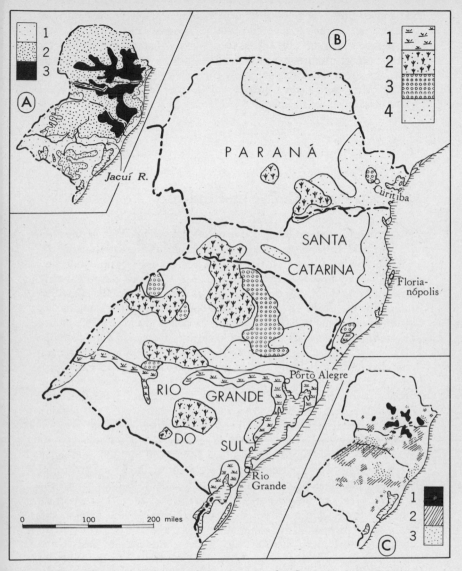

A. *Generalized relief (in feet above mean sea level):* 1—0 to 656; 2—656 to 2,625; 3—2,625 and above

B. *Major crop areas:* 1—irrigated rice; 2—wheat (generally in association with other crops); 3—vineyards (generally in association with cereals and other crops); 4—other cropland

C. *European colonization:* 1—Slavs; 2—Germans; 3—Italians

São Paulo, but is beginning to turn toward Paraná's own capital of Curitiba, one of the most modern and prosperous cities of Brazil, with a population nearing 500,000. Today, western Paraná still affords the country's most promising agricultural frontier, while the state has already surpassed São Paulo in coffee production. With the family farm as the basic unit, Paraná helps provide the "dynamic stability" of which Brazil has such a need.

53. São Paulo: Coffee and Industry

By far the most important and dynamic single component of the Brazilian federal union is the state of São Paulo, the greatest industrial center in the hemisphere outside the United States. In population and wealth São Paulo alone dwarfs most Latin American countries; only Mexico, Argentina, and Colombia are as populous as the Brazilian state, with its nearly 16 million inhabitants. Located on a plateau at an altitude of about 2,300 feet, it enjoys a uniformly favorable climate; the *paulistas* are a sturdy mixture of essentially European ethnic strains.

The development of São Paulo to its present position of primacy took place only during the last century. Quite simply, São Paulo provided over two-thirds of the country's coffee at a time when Brazil was meeting as much as three-fourths of the world demand for this commodity. The vast proceeds from this trade underwrote the region's industrialization, and largely financed the federal government.

The closing years of the nineteenth century saw São Paulo take its great leap forward. Population doubled from 1885 to 1900, and again in the ensuing twenty years. Some three-fifths of the heavy stream of European immigrants settled in São Paulo, chiefly as laborers on the coffee fazendas. A railroad network was built, second in Latin America only to that reaching out from Buenos Aires through the Pampa, and this was supplemented by all-weather highways. São Paulo's port of Santos developed rapidly into one of the continent's busiest. Gross overproduction of coffee paved the way for disaster when the effects of the world depression hit Brazil in 1930, and in the postwar period the effects of Colombian, Central American, and, more recently, African competition have been strongly felt in Brazil. Nonetheless, coffee has continued to be Brazil's main source of foreign exchange. In 1964, it provided $800 million of the country's $1.5 billion foreign-exchange earnings.

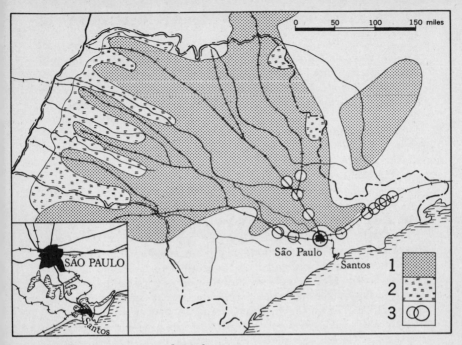

1—coffee; 2—cotton; 3—industrial cities

Since 1930, great changes have taken place in São Paulo. Small farms multiplied as large landowners sold off portions of their estates for capital to invest in industry and urban real estate. Spurred by the Japanese immigrants, cotton became the chief money crop on the São Paulo agricultural frontier. São Paulo agriculture has become increasingly diversified and mechanized. But the most dramatic transformation has taken place in the urban areas. The establishment of manufacturing pushed the population of São Paulo city (a provincial town of 35,000 in 1883 and 340,000 in 1907) over the 1 million mark in 1930 and, with its suburbs, past the 5-million mark today. In the last decade, São Paulo has developed as one of the world's major automotive centers, and modern steel mills and oil refineries are situated in nearby Cubatão on the way to Santos, itself a city of more than 300,000.

54. Rio de Janeiro and Its Mineral-Rich Hinterland

Equally as important to the life of the nation as São Paulo is the Brazilian East, comprised chiefly of the states of Guanabara, Rio de Janeiro, and Minas Gerais. With a relatively urbanized population of nearly 20 million, this region contains much of Brazil's industry and most of its great mineral wealth. Greater Rio de Janeiro (Guanabara and the surrounding portion of Rio de Janeiro state) is a metropolitan area with close to 5 million inhabitants. Although the legal capital was moved to Brasília in 1960, most of the bureaucracy remains in "Rio," which is also the country's chief port and unchallenged cultural capital. As a manufacturing center, it runs a strong second to São Paulo.

The importance of this region came rather late in the colonial period with the discovery of gold in Minas Gerais (General Mines) in 1698. For a century "Minas" flourished as the world's most important producer of gold and a major supplier of diamonds. Emigrants flocked in from the declining Northeast, and Rio de Janeiro prospered as the region's port. In 1763 it replaced Salvador as Brazil's capital, and as a result of the Napoleonic Wars became the seat of the Portuguese Empire in 1808. The region went into temporary decline during the nineteenth century as easily accessible gold deposits gave out. Farming and particularly the raising of livestock came to be the basis of the region's economy.

In recent decades, the development of vast iron reserves has again brought mining to the fore. Near Belo Horizonte—founded as the capital of Minas Gerais in 1896 and now a city of some 800,000—are found whole mountains of iron comprising nearly one-fourth of the world's known reserves. Brazil has been cautious about permitting large-scale foreign exploitation of this very high-quality ore, but has exported significant quantities through a government agency. By 1964, iron ore was the country's third-ranking export. Brazil has eagerly pressed ahead with the creation of Latin America's leading steel industry. The National Steel Company, better known as Volta Redonda, was a product of wartime U.S. assistance to Brazil. Although its production has been raised to some 2 million tons a year, it will soon be matched by the production of the newer Paulista Steel Company (COSIPA) and a Minas Gerais enterprise, USIMINAS. Manganese, chromium, nickel, tungsten, quartz crystals, and industrial diamonds are also found in abundance in this area. Although local coal and oil are in relatively short supply, very large modern hydroelectric projects such as Furnas and Três Marias have helped to break open the power bottleneck.

While Minas Gerais, whose population of 11 million is second only to São Paulo, has remained a bastion of moderate conservatism and the

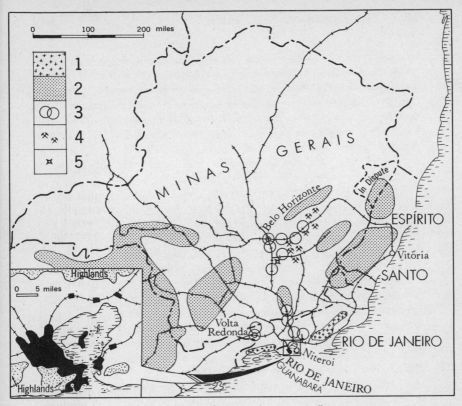

1—bananas; *2*—coffee; *3*—industrial cities; *4*—iron ore; *5*—manganese

major single source of strength for center-right political parties, the metropolis of Rio de Janeiro has been the scene of considerable political unrest in recent years. Communist and other extremist elements have made far greater headway among organized labor and student groups here than in stable São Paulo. Perhaps 750,000 of Rio de Janeiro's inhabitants live in the hillside slums, or *favelas*, which infest the city. The anti-Communist but reform-minded Guanabara Governor Carlos Lacerda, with considerable Alliance for Progress financial assistance, has done much to ameliorate serious housing, health, education, water, and transportation problems. Nevertheless, squeezed by inflation, the politically important lower middle class and the masses of workers are restless.

55. The Brazilian Northeast

In marked contrast to the region below Minas Gerais and Bahia, where the level of economic development matches that of southern and central, if not northern, Europe, the Northeast of Brazil constitutes one of the major depressed areas of the hemisphere. Unlike the sparsely settled Amazonian region, this part of Brazil is densely populated and has played a major role in the development of the nation. Pernambuco and Bahia were the key colonial centers for over 250 years, and the region's population of nearly 25 million still exceeds that of Argentina or of Peru, Ecuador, and Bolivia combined.

The Northeast itself is a very diverse area. The narrow coastal zone which receives adequate rainfall is the most densely inhabited and contains the major cities of Recife (900,000), Salvador (750,000), and Fortaleza (600,000). Inland areas are subject to periodic droughts which force great numbers to flee to the cities or to migrate to the South. Other population shifts have been toward the frontier areas of western Maranhão and upper Goiás, where agricultural development affords a potentially significant means of reducing the region's critical population pressures. Bahia, lying chiefly to the south and east of the Rio São Francisco, plays a unique role in the life of the nation. Larger and more populous than half the Latin American countries, Bahia produces most of Brazil's cacao, tobacco, and sugar. More important, it contains the country's only major producing oilfield.

The Brazilian Northeast is certainly one of the most critical and potentially explosive areas in the hemisphere. The cities have been unable to absorb the thousands of refugees from the interior, who remain a restless and discontented mass, and the peasantry in the crowded coastal belt has awakened politically during the past decade. Extremist agitators built up significant followings. The best known of these are Francisco Julião, a Marxist who became a Federal Deputy, and pro-Communist Miguel Arraes, elected Mayor of Recife in 1959 and Governor of Pernambuco three years later.

Recognition of the seriousness of the situation in the Northeast came slowly to the Rio de Janeiro– and São Paulo–oriented elements dominant in the national government. The catastrophic drought of 1958 and the blatant inadequacy of graft- and politics-ridden relief programs led to the establishment of an area-wide development agency, the Superintendency for the Economic Development of the Northeast (SUDENE). Under the Alliance for Progress, the United States in 1961 pledged at least $131 million to the first stage of SUDENE's multifaceted programs. Although a number of badly needed steps have been taken, po-

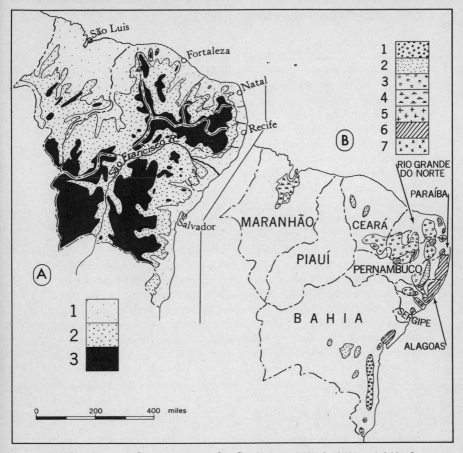

A. *Relief (in feet above mean sea level)*: *1*—0 to 656; *2*—656 to 1,640; *3*—above 1,640

B. *Major specialty crop areas*: *1*—cocoa; *2*—coffee; *3*—cotton; *4*—rice; *5*—sisal; *6*—sugar; *7*—tobacco

litical differences have hamstrung SUDENE. Celso Furtado, its first director, became Goulart's Minister of Planning and subsequently a political exile. President Castelo Branco, a native of the Northeast, is aware of the magnitude of the problems there and of the need for effective action, but so far priority has been given to stabilization.

56.   The Amazon: Boom and Bust

The Brazilian North is dominated by the Amazon, one of the world's great rivers. Comprising over two-fifths of the country (or nearly 1.4 million square miles), this region contains only 4 per cent of its population. The main area of concentrated settlement is near Belém, the eighth largest city in Brazil, with about 450,000 inhabitants. Although much of the Amazon region is covered by tropical rain forest (selva), it is not entirely unsuited to settlement and offers a potential escape valve for hemispheric overpopulation. The climate is rainy and hot, but not unbearably so. Indeed, it is the monotony of the climate that Europeans find most disagreeable, rather than the temperature, which is in the same range as that of Puerto Rico, Panama, or Jamaica. The Amazon and several of its major tributaries are navigable for hundreds of miles; many ocean-going ships can reach the docks of Manaus, more than 1,000 miles from the Atlantic, with little difficulty. Smaller cargo vessels regularly continue another thousand miles upriver to Iquitos in Peru. Yet as long as other large virgin areas remain to be settled in Brazil, development of the North will be delayed.

The Amazon region did enjoy a significant spurt of development during the period from 1850 to 1910, when the world demand for wild rubber shot up. Workers were hurriedly drawn in from the excess labor force of the Northeast, and fortunes were made in land speculation. Culture, in the form of a magnificent opera house and European theatrical stars, came to Manaus. But the bubble burst soon after the turn of the century, when seeds from Brazilian trees were used to start rubber plantations in the East Indies. From the dominant position in 1910, Brazil in two years lost nearly all the world market. An effort begun in 1927 by the Ford Motor Company to establish rubber plantations along an Amazon tributary faltered in the face of labor shortages and improved techniques for making synthetic rubber, and in 1946 the Fordlandia and Belterra concessions were turned back to the Brazilian Government. At present, then, this vast region contributes very little to the life of the nation. Brazil nuts, pepper, rice, and jute (the latter products of recent Japanese immigrants) are the basis of limited commercial agriculture. Since 1956, a major manganese mine in the territory of Amapá provides ore for export and relative prosperity for the limited population of the area. But in many respects contraband may well be the major industry of the region. Certainly it is at the base of several individual fortunes and a major source of income for many politicians.

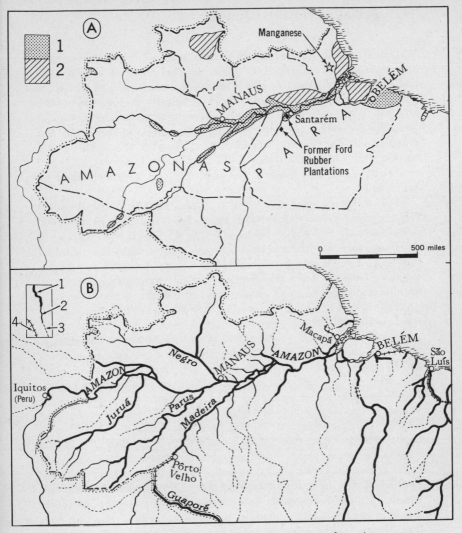

A. *Political divisions and major use areas:* 1—crop agriculture (rice, cocoa, jute, tobacco, etc.); 2—cattle ranching

B. *Major means of transport:* 1—navigable river, regularly used; 2—navigable river, seldom used; 3—non-navigable river; 4—railroad

57. Brasília and the Frontier

Well inward from the densely populated heart of Brazil lies the area known as the Central-West—the great wooded plains of Mato Grosso and Goiás. Development of this interior has long been a Brazilian national aspiration, but until recent years relatively little has been done about it. With population pressures becoming acute in the Northeast, a rapidly developing southern frontier, and interior Minas Gerais and Bahia slowly filling up, the "march toward the west" may soon become a major factor in Brazil's national life. At present, however, this is still essentially an area of open range with only scattered towns and no major cities.

Most of this region of over 700,000 square miles lies at nearly 4,000 feet above sea level and enjoys hot, rainy summers combined with cool, dry winters. Scrub woodlands and savannas are interspersed with semideciduous forests. Although some commercial agriculture is established around Campo Grande in southern Mato Grosso, extensive ranching is the rule. Some iron ore and manganese are shipped out from Corumbá, an important river port and railhead on the Bolivian border. Nearer to population centers, the lower portion of Goiás has begun to be developed during the last two decades.

Transfer of the nation's capital from Rio de Janeiro to the interior has been sanctioned by the Constitution ever since establishment of the Republic. But not until 1956, when Juscelino Kubitschek became President, was anything actually done to make this dream a reality. Kubitschek had served as Mayor and Governor in Belo Horizonte, itself an "artificial" capital constructed at the end of the last century. In 1957 he obtained congressional approval for construction of the new capital, and less than three years later, on April 21, 1960, the official transfer of government to Brasília was made amidst international publicity. Located between Goiânia and the Minas Gerais border, the new Federal District lies nearly 600 miles north of Rio de Janeiro. Although construction has been slowed down since 1961, it now contains nearly 200,000 persons out of a planned eventual population of a half million. Well served by air, it is also linked to Belo Horizonte and Rio de Janeiro by a major highway; the rest of the ambitious road network started by Kubitschek, with Brasília at its hub, is still incomplete. It is not yet clear whether Brasília will eventually justify its great cost, felt throughout Brazil in the form of accentuated inflation.

Industrialization, which has in recent decades replaced agricultural expansion as the principal force orienting the Brazilian economy, now shapes internal political and economic trends as well as international

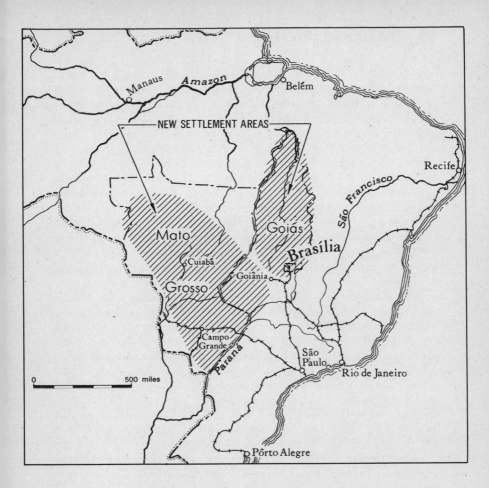

trade relationships. The growth of industry has given industrialists new political influence, sharply diminishing the preeminence once enjoyed by the coffee planters. The concentration of industry in the urban centers of the Southeast has further reinforced the dominant position of this area. At the same time, the middle class has established itself as a major political force. As a result of the concentration of a large laboring population in the industrial centers and a rapid increase in the educational facilities available to workers, the urban working class has also begun to make its influence felt in the government.

58. Politics in Brazil

Brazil is a federal republic composed of twenty-two states, a Federal District and four territories, with a Presidential system similar to that of the United States. Its political life is distinguished by the multiplicity of political parties of recent origin, the relative lack of ideological distinctions among them, and the highly personalistic nature of political leadership. All of the thirteen legally registered parties were founded after the fall of the Vargas dictatorship in 1945, and only three are organized on a nationwide basis. The others are essentially regional, with the bulk of their membership concentrated in a few states. The personal element predominates over questions of program and policy in virtually every party. Neither the professional politicians nor the voters have as yet developed a strong sense of party loyalty and shift allegiance as it suits their personal convenience. Consequently, a party's strength or weakness at the polls usually reflects the popularity of the individual candidate rather than that of the party platform.

Although each party has adopted a formal program its position on specific issues is frequently determined by short-range political considerations. Even the differences between parties at opposite ends of the political spectrum are usually overshadowed by the qualities all parties share in common. In varying degrees, each appeals to and reflects the highly developed nationalism which in recent years has become acute among vocal sectors of the population, particularly the urban middle- and industrial working-class representatives. The Brazilian Labor Party, long headed by Goulart, has gone the farthest in this direction, but the leaders of its leftist wing were stripped of their political rights following the April, 1964, revolution. The Social Democratic Party and the National Democratic Union, the two other major parties, are both essentially center-right in their orientation. The former has generally been in power since 1946, while the latter has been the backbone of the opposition. At present, they are generally cooperating with the Castelo Branco government.

Regardless of party, Brazilian politicians increasingly court the middle- and working-class electorates. As a result, the locus of political power has been shifting from the economic aristocracy in alliance with the military hierarchy to the urban middle class supported by urban laboring groups. A majority of policy-making positions and legislative posts are held by professional men and representatives of the powerful urban industrial, financial, and business interests. However, the new generation of political leaders and government officials are more representative of the middle class. Moreover, despite the literacy requirement which disenfranchises almost half the adult population of Brazil,

States (with capital cities), territories, and the Federal District. Areas too small to be named on map:

States: 1—Rio Grande do Norte; 2—Paraíba; 3—Pernambuco; 4—Alagoas; 5—Sergipe; 6—Espirito Santo; 7—Rio de Janeiro; 8—Guanabara; 9—Federal District

Territories: 10—Rondonia; 11—Roraima; 12—Amapá; 13—Fernando de Noronha

the popular base of the government is steadily expanding. Approximately 7.5 million Brazilians voted in the 1950 general elections, a new record for Brazil, and by 1962 the figure had doubled.

59.   Pan-American Unity

Although there is substantial diversity in Latin America and the region is divided into nearly thirty political units, there are also certain basic features and forces making for unity. During the colonial era, most of the area was under Spanish or Portuguese rule, and the two mother countries were themselves united during part of this period. All but a few of these countries gained their independence at about the same time, largely through cooperative effort. The Roman Catholic Church long dominated educational and cultural as well as religious life, and most of the people remain faithful to their Latin Catholic heritage.

Latin America has been relatively free of wars, and few territorial conflicts or bitter rivalries persist down to the present. The inter-American system, begun in 1889 with the establishment of the Pan American Union, gradually evolved as a viable regional organization. Tensions within the system, resulting in large part from U.S. military interventions in the Caribbean areas, were greatly reduced in the 1930's by the "Good Neighbor Policy" of the Roosevelt Administration and U.S. agreement to accept the principle of nonintervention as embodied in a series of inter-American treaties. In this manner a very high degree of hemispheric solidarity was achieved by the outbreak of World War II, and a Brazilian expeditionary force fought on the side of the allies in the Italian campaign. Argentina, however, was recalcitrant. The defeat of the Axis reduced the so-called "Argentina problem," and the basis for an effective system of collective security was established through the Inter-American Treaty of Reciprocal Assistance (Rio Pact) of 1947. The following year, at Bogotá, the Organization of American States (OAS) came into being as a regional organization in keeping with the Charter of the United Nations, in whose drafting the Latin American countries had played a significant role.

Latin American dissatisfaction over the halting response of the United States to their aspirations and needs in the field of economic development came to a head in 1958 and 1959; the Eisenhower Administration belatedly came forth with a more positive program the following year. By the time of the Act of Bogotá in September, 1960, however, the Cuban problem (*see Map 25*) was dividing hemisphere opinion and arousing new passions. The Alliance for Progress, proposed by the Kennedy Administration in the spring of 1961 and launched at Punta del Este the following August, called for a joint attack upon problems of underdevelopment in Latin America and committed the United States to heavy sustained financial assistance, amounting to $20

1—Central American Common Market; 2—Latin American Free Trade Area

million over a decade, to those countries which undertook certain basic reforms and the total mobilization of their own resources. During the first four years of the Alliance, significant, although spotty, progress was made along these lines, and the long-run outcome of this vital undertaking remains in doubt.

60.   Population Pressure

Latin America has the highest sustained rate of population growth of any major area of the world. For the region as a whole, the annual increase is above 2.5 per cent, but by country it ranges from below 1.5 to over 3.5 per cent. Thus, while total Latin American population can be expected to double in just over twenty-five years, in some countries this will take twenty years, in others thirty, and in a few much longer. One major implication of this wide variation is in economic growth rates. To achieve the annual per capita gain of 2.5 per cent specified by the Charter of Punta del Este, some nations will need to expand their economies nearly twice as rapidly as others, with the greater part of the increment serving merely to keep abreast of population growth. As of 1965, the population of the region is estimated at 245 million, with one-third of these living in Brazil, one-sixth in Mexico, and another one-sixth in Argentina and Colombia combined. More than half the population are under eighteen years of age. By the turn of the century, the region's inhabitants should number 600 million. This figure could be raised even higher by better public-health facilities and higher living standards. Under these conditions, economic progress will continue to be difficult; shortages in housing and in schools will be particularly hard to overcome.

Although vast areas of the South American continent are sparsely populated, pressure upon land and food supplies will focus attention upon their development during the 1970's and 1980's. Technological advances will facilitate utilization of the less fertile lands, but sheer necessity will be a major factor. At the same time, urbanization will continue apace, with many provincial centers becoming major cities and the great metropolitan areas, such as Mexico City, Buenos Aires, São Paulo, Santiago, and Lima, adding millions to their populations. Thus, the area will be faced for many years with the manifold problems of rapid urban growth, in most cases substantially exceeding the rate of industrialization. Wise national leadership and continued heavy technical and economic assistance from the United States and other free-world countries will be necessary for some time to come if the countries of the region are to provide higher living standards, greater security, and increased freedom for rapidly growing populations. With $1.2 billion of U.S. official assistance in 1964, Latin America achieved a per capita rise in gross national product of nearly 3 per cent, the highest in recent years. Sustained over the rest of the decade, this would meet the minimum goals of the Alliance.

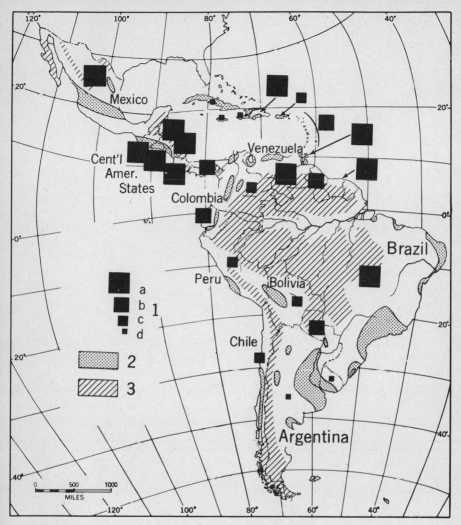

1—rate of population increase (by countries): a—3.0–4.0; b—2.5–3.0; c—2.0–2.5; d—1.2–2.0; 2—heavily populated area; 3—sparsely populated area

Index

Index*

* The numbers refer to map numbers and accompanying text, not to pages.